ANSIBLE
for IT EXPERTS

Denis Zuev,
Artemii Kropachev
and
Dmitrii Mostovshchikov

Contents

Preface

Hello everyone,

Before you start reading any further, I want to tell you that this book is intended to teach you some Ansible basics and get you started in your automation journey. I hope that once you finished reading this book, it plants the seed and eventually grows up to something more and eventually change your mindset. Because it changed mine. I and my colleagues want to share that experience with you, and get you started with Ansible and Automation in general.

I am getting a lot of messages on a daily basis from people with networking background via emails, texts, linkedin, skype asking me about what to next, where is it all going, how do I start with Linux, Automation or DevOps, and all other sort of questions. And I always tell them that Automation is the key and the future, do not be afraid to start doing it right now, be ready to step out your comfort zone and deep dive into it. Good luck! .

Denis Zuev, 12/20/2017

Introduction

This book is intended to share our experience and approach in Automating your infrastructure with Ansible. We are extremely technical and practical people, and that is why we cover just a little bit of theory and give you more practical examples.

There is a lot of examples and exercises around the topics and challenges we think you might face during your Automation journey.

To help you pick the starting point, below is a brief chapter-by-chapter description of this book.

Chapter 1 explains what Git is and how it may help you during your Automation journey.

Chapter 2 gives you basic information about Vagrant and how to build your lab environment. We use Vagrant with virtualbox/kvm in this book to speed up bringing up your lab environment. You can use other virtualization platforms for your lab, if you know what you are going.

Chapter 3 main chapter about Ansible. We have plenty of examples here based on what we use on a daily basis. Remember, that practice is the key to success.

Chapter 4 gives some tips and tricks which you can use while working with Ansible on a daily basis. That should keep you out of troubles for some time.

Prerequisites

Before you begin, we want to make sure that you have everything in place. You will need a PC with at least 8GB of RAM and at least 20GB of free disk space. CPU is not that relevant, but make sure you have some CPU resources available for a better performance. OS is not that relevant since Vagrant will run on majority of operating systems. But in this book, we use MacOS 10.12, Ubuntu 16.04 and Centos 7.4.

We also assume that our readers have basic understanding of Linux-like operating systems.

About the Authors

Denis Zuev is a passionate IT expert with more than 10 years of experience. Throughout his career he has taken development, pre-sales, architect, and managerial roles in small to international size projects with the main focus in networking. Several years back he started working with SDN, Open Source, Automation and DevOps and Programming and this is what he spends most of his time nowadays. Denis is also known for his professional and certification achievements. At the moment of writing this book he holds following industry expert level certifications: RHCA, CCIE, JNCIE, CCDE, HCIE, VCIX-NV.

Dmitrii Mostovshchikov has been working in the IT for last 15 years with the main focus on open source technologies. He started working with FreeBSD in the University back in 2001. It showed him how powerful Open Source is. He started as Systems Admin and continued as Developer and System Architect. Few years ago he switched and deep dived into Virtualization, Clouds, Containers, Automation, and DevOps technologies and products. He is an eager learner especially when it comes to Open Source related technologies and products. Dmitrii is also a Red Hat Certified Architect Level 9 and holds a lot of other excellence certificates by Red Hat.

Artemii Kropachev is a passionate IT expert with more than 15 years experience with Linux and Open Source in general. He started as a Pascal/Delphi developer for scientific programs in 1998 and moved to perl/c/php to development and FreeBSD system administration in 2002. He has done a lot of Linux, Oracle Solaris, IBM AIX, HP-UX, *BSD projects as well as building IaaS/PaaS/SaaS clouds with high level of automation based on the following technologies: OpenStack, AWS, OpenShift, Kubernetes, Ansible, Chef, Puppet. Artemii is one of the most certified Red Hat Certified Architects in the word. Currently his certification status is Red Hat Certified Architect Level 17.

Chapter 1. Git

Why Git

We were looking for a tool which allows us to provide a better experience with our readers. It had to be popular, easy to learn and free to use. Since we are using Git, the choice is very obvious. For those who is unfamiliar with Git, we hope that you will learn more about it in this chapter and start using it on a daily basis.

About Git

Git is a distributed version control system developed as a storage for source code and tracking changes. This is an absolutely free software distributed under General Public License (GPL). Git allows a number of people work on same projects independently, share their progress with other people all around the world.

Git is a very simple yet powerful tool that has been actively used by developers, engineering, DevoOs and other communities for years. Git is not a main topic of this book, so we are going to cover enough for you to get started with Git and share all Ansible and Vagrant we use in this book.

Installing Git

Installing Git is quite easy. Below are 3 examples for different operating systems we used to write this book.

Git is available on almost every Linux distributive and also on Solaris, FreeBSD, Windows, Mac OS X and many other systems.

MacOS X

```
$ brew install git
```

CentOS

```
$ sudo yum install -y git
```

Ubuntu

```
$ sudo apt install -y git
```

Verify that Git was installed on your system

```
$ git --version
git version 2.13.0
```

Cloning github repository

Download the repo from github.com. It includes all the necessary file we will need later for this book. If you feel uncomfortable at any point while reading this book, you can refer to it. The folder structure is quite intuitive, so you should not have any problems finding the right solution.

```
$ mkdir repos; cd repos
$ git clone \
https://github.com/flashdumper/ansible_book.git
$ cd ansible_book
```

That is what you need from Git for this book. We are going to work with Git on a few more topics to give you an idea about how you can use it on your daily basis.

Creating an own Git repository

Git allows creating local repositories to keep your code under version control and share your experience with the others. Get yourself registered on http://github.com. It should be fairly easy and straightforward process.

Once you are done:

1. Press "+" and then "New repository" at the top-right corner of github webpage
2. Specify Repository Name, like "my_project1"
3. Leave the rest of the settings by default and then press "Create Repository" button.

For more information, follow the link: https://help.github.com/ articles/ create-a-repo/

At this point you are ready to clone your own repository. Copy the URL that that should look like this "git clone https://github.com/<your_username>/ my_project1.git".

```
$ mkdir repos; cd repos
$ git clone \
https://github.com/<your _username>/my _project1.git

Cloning into 'my _project1'...
warning: You appear to have cloned an empty
repository.
```

Configuring Git

Before you start working with git repositories, we need to define our email and username. This minimal configuration is required to start working with Git:

```
$ git config --global user.name "Your Name"
$ git config --global user.email \
```

```
$ git config --global push.default simple
```

More configuration options available by typing the command git config --help or man git-config.

Git architecture

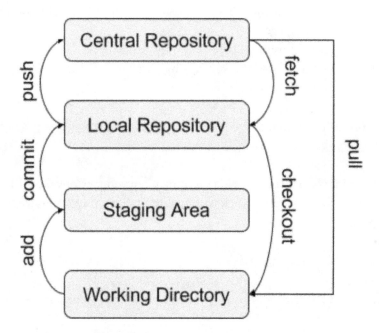

Git consists of 4 main components:

- Central Repository - it is a metadata and object database shared with other users. Central repository examples are github, bitbucket, gitlab, etc.
- Local Repository - complete clone of your central repository that is being copied to your local PC.
- Staging Area - is an abstraction layer where, where Git starts tracking the changes.
- Working directory - is the directory where you make all the modifications on your local PC. Changes are not under version control and untracked.

Git basics

The most common operations which performed while working with files under Git control are:

- add, delete, update files to staging area
- commit files to local repository
- pushing and pulling changes while working with central repository
- rolling back the changes.

Using Git help

At any point of time, do not be shy to use git help if you do not understand a Git command, subcommand or key option.

```
$ git --help
usage: git [--version] [--help] [-c name=value]
           [--exec-path[=<path>]] [--html-path]
[--man-path] [--info-path]
           [-p|--paginate|--no-pager] [--no-replace-
objects] [--bare]
           [--git-dir=<path>] [--work-tree=<path>]
[--namespace=<name>]
           <command> [<args>]


The most commonly used git commands are:
   add        Add file contents to the index
   bisect     Find by binary search the change that
introduced a bug
   branch     List, create, or delete branches
   checkout   Checkout a branch or paths to the
working tree
   clone      Clone a repository into a new
directory
   commit     Record changes to the repository
...
output truncated for brevity
```

```
...
'git help -a' and 'git help -g' lists available
subcommands and some
concept guides. See 'git help <command>' or 'git
help <concept>'
to read about a specific subcommand or concept.

$ git commit -h
usage: git commit [options] [--] <pathspec>...
    -q, --quiet              suppress summary after
successful commit
    -v, --verbose            show diff in commit
message template

Commit message options
    -F, --file <file>       read message from file
...
output truncated for brevity
...

Commit contents options
    -a, --all               commit all changed files
    -i, --include           add specified files to index
for commit
  ...
output truncated for brevity
  ...
```

Working with Git

When you begin a new project, it is a good idea to create a git repository first and keep working in that directory. If you already have a project not under version control, you can simply move these files to git repository.

Let's create a text file with simple content.

```
$ cd ~/repos/my_project1
$ echo This is our first project > README.md
```

Check the status of README.md

```
$ git status .
# On branch master
#
# Initial commit
#
# Untracked files:
#   (use "git add <file>..." to include in what will
be committed)
#
#       README.md
nothing added to commit but untracked files present
(use "git add" to track)
```

Note that README.md is under "Untracked files". Now add the README.
md file for tracking by Git.

```
#add README.md file specifically
$ git add README.md
```
or
```
#add all the new or changed files in this repo
$ git add .
```

Check the status of your Git repo

```
$ git status

# On branch master
#
# Initial commit
#
# Changes to be committed:
#   (use "git rm --cached <file>..." to unstage)
#
#       new file:   README.md
#
```

Note that README.me file appears under "Changes to be committed". The "git add" command just updates the repository index and prepares the content for next commit. At this point README.md file is added to "staging area" on your PC. Staging area is basically the directory you are working in.

Now, move README.md to the local repo

```
$ git commit -m 'First Commit'
[master (root-commit) 5d62cb9] First Commit
 1 file changed, 1 insertion(+)
 create mode 100644 README.md
```

Check repo status

```
$ git status

# On branch master
nothing to commit, working directory clean
```

Command output tells you that there is nothing to commit because README.md is at the same state as the one in local repo. Do not be confused, README.md is still just in the repo on your PC, and not being pushed to upstream repo (github.com in our case).

Now edit README.md

```
$ echo README.me File is modified >> README.md
$ cat README.md

This is our first project
README.me File is modified
```

Check repo status

```
$ git status

# On branch master
# Changes not staged for commit:
```

```
#     (use "git add <file>..." to update what will be
committed)
#     (use "git checkout -- <file>..." to discard
changes in working directory)
#
#          modified:    README.md
#
no changes added to commit (use "git add" and/or
"git commit -a")
```

Note that Git identified changes in README.md.
To apply the changes in the repo we need to run "git add" and "git commit"
again.

```
$ git add README.md
$ git status

# On branch master
# Changes to be committed:
#     (use "git reset HEAD <file>..." to unstage)
#
#          modified:    README.md
#

$git commit -m 'Second Commit'

[master 97695b4] README.md modified
 1 file changed, 2 insertions(+), 1 deletion(-)
```

Check what Git knows about the lasts actions

```
$ git log

commit 97695b4fe57c03932887d23497aac3f7febc1289
Author: Your Name <you@example.com>
Date:    Mon Sep 25 07:43:15 2017 +0000


     Second Commit
```

```
commit 5d62cb978f9e5441d2d4913c7c0ff294992b567d
Author: Your Name <you@example.com>
Date:    Mon Sep 25 07:20:18 2017 +0000

    First Commit
```

At this point git knows about the changes made to README.md. There were two commits with comments "First commit" and "Second Commit". You can also check who did these changes at what time.

You can also check the list of files stored in your local repo with the following command:

```
$ git ls-files -s

100644 4acbdbe4e8d334035c9bb94cdf7a4c2ce945e7fb
0       README.md
```

At this point of time we have been working with the git repo locally on our PC. Let's push README.md to github.com

```
$ git push

Username for 'https://github.com': flashdumper
Password for 'https://flashdumper@github.com':
Counting objects: 6, done.
Compressing objects: 100% (3/3), done.
Writing objects: 100% (6/6), 510 bytes | 0 bytes/s, done.
Total 6 (delta 0), reused 0 (delta 0)
To https://github.com/flashdumper/my__project1.git
 * [new branch]      master -> master
```

README.md fine was committed to github.com. What now? Now let's remove README.md from our PC.

```
$ rm -f README.md
```

```
$ ls -l
total 0
```

It is where it will get a bit confusing. README.md deleted physically from your PC, but it is still in your local git repo.

Just to note that README.md file now stored in 3 different places:

1. Local directory (local directory)
2. In local git repo (stage area)
3. On github.com (upstream)

Check git status

```
$ git status
# On branch master
# Changes not staged for commit:
#    (use "git add/rm <file>..." to update what will be
committed)
#    (use "git checkout -- <file>..." to discard
changes in working directory)
#
#       deleted:     README.md
#
no changes added to commit (use "git add" and/or
"git commit -a")
```

The status of README.md is deleted. Note that output says that to revert the changes we can use "git checkout -- <file>" command.

Let's try it out.

```
$ git checkout README.md

$ ls -l
total 4
-rw-r--r--. 1 root root 53 Sep 25 08:32 README.md
```

```
$ cat README.md
This is our first project
README.me File is modified
```

As you can see README.md with all its content is back. Isn't it cool? Delete README.md and commit the change. That is an advanced topic but useful to know in case if you run into the situation like that.

```
$ git rm README.md
rm 'README.md'

$ git status
# On branch master
# Changes to be committed:
#    (use "git reset HEAD <file>..." to unstage)
#
#        deleted:      README.md
#

$ git commit -m '3rd commit, README.md deleted'
[master 60e167c] README.md deleted
 1 file changed, 2 deletions(-)
 delete mode 100644 README.md

$ git log
commit 2b0afc3e15f9fb9b3b86731cd3bb3134b33319eb
Author: Your Name <your@email.com>
Date:    Sun Oct 15 01:54:08 2017 +0000

    3rd commit, README.md deleted

commit 8d72fb1f3c4a59c94d5cd99746a9ab83332cdf45
Author: Your Name <your@email.com>
Date:    Sun Oct 15 01:28:07 2017 +0000

    Second Commit
```

```
commit e6761aea31b2a9af5a48a0013ca345c3e8adbe0d
Author: Your Name <your@email.com>
Date:     Sun Oct 15 01:26:52 2017 +0000

    First Commit

$ ls -l
total 0
```

Change has been submitted to local repo and get README.md file is back.
We won't be getting into details, but rather show you the way to make it
happen in case if you run into situation like that.

```
$ git reflog
2b0afc3 HEAD@{0}: commit: 3rd commit, README.md deleted
8d72fb1 HEAD@{1}: commit: Second Commit
e6761ae HEAD@{2}: commit (initial): First Commit

$ git reset --hard 8d72fb1
HEAD is now at 8d72fb1 Second Commit

$ ls -l
total 4
-rw-r--r--. 1 root root 53 Oct 15 02:07 README.md
```

Viola! We have README.md back.

Another quick way of doing it is with "git checkout" and "git merge"
commands.

```
$ git log
commit 2b0afc3e15f9fb9b3b86731cd3bb3134b33319eb
Author: Your Name <your@email.com>
Date:     Sun Oct 15 01:54:08 2017 +0000
```

3rd commit, README.md deleted

```
commit 8d72fb1f3c4a59c94d5cd99746a9ab83332cdf45
Author: Your Name <your@email.com>
Date:    Sun Oct 15 01:28:07 2017 +0000

    Second Commit

commit e6761aea31b2a9af5a48a0013ca345c3e8adbe0d
Author: Your Name <your@email.com>
Date:    Sun Oct 15 01:26:52 2017 +0000

    First Commit

$ git checkout
8d72fb1f3c4a59c94d5cd99746a9ab83332cdf45
Note: checking out
'8d72fb1f3c4a59c94d5cd99746a9ab83332cdf45'.
…
output truncated for brevity
…
HEAD is now at 8d72fb1... Second Commit

$ git merge -s ours master
Merge made by the 'ours' strategy.

Press ":wq" combination If you have been redirected
to vi editor.

$ git checkout master
Warning: you are leaving 1 commit behind, not
connected to
any of your branches:

  6a62a40 Merge branch 'master' into HEAD

If you want to keep them by creating a new branch,
this may be a good time to do so with:
```

```
git branch new __branch __name 6a62a40

Switched to branch 'master'
Your branch is ahead of 'origin/master' by 1 commit.
  (use "git push" to publish your local commits)

$ git merge 6a62a40
Updating 2b0afc3..6a62a40
Fast-forward
 README.md | 2 ++
 1 file changed, 2 insertions(+)
 create mode 100644 README.md

$ ls -l
total 4
-rw-r--r--. 1 root root 153 Sep 25 19:48 README.md
```

And check the git log for making sure that the changes were added into the repository.

```
$ git log
commit 6a62a4077a38a85134f883e46810dfcf0540d969
Merge: 8d72fb1 2b0afc3
Author: Your Name <your@email.com>
Date:    Sun Oct 15 02:17:22 2017 +0000

    Merge branch 'master' into HEAD

commit 2b0afc3e15f9fb9b3b86731cd3bb3134b33319eb
Author: Your Name <your@email.com>
Date:    Sun Oct 15 01:54:08 2017 +0000

    3rd commit, README.md deleted

commit 8d72fb1f3c4a59c94d5cd99746a9ab83332cdf45
Author: Your Name <your@email.com>
Date:    Sun Oct 15 01:28:07 2017 +0000
```

Second Commit

commit e6761aea31b2a9af5a48a0013ca345c3e8adbe0d
Author: Your Name <your@email.com>
Date: Sun Oct 15 01:26:52 2017 +0000

First Commit

Chapter 2. Vagrant

About Vagrant

From www.vagrantup.com "Vagrant provides the same, easy workflow regardless of your role as a developer, operator, or designer. It leverages a declarative configuration file which describes all your software requirements, packages, operating system configuration, users, and more."

Why Vagrant

We also need a tool that allows our readers to bring their environments up quick and easy.

And Vagrant is a great fit because:

- It is free
- Easy to learn and use
- Quick to tear down and bring up again
- Integration with Ansible
- Easy to use CLI

It does not mean that you can not use other tools, but we found that Vagrant is the most usable and easiest among the other ones.

Vagrant Architecture

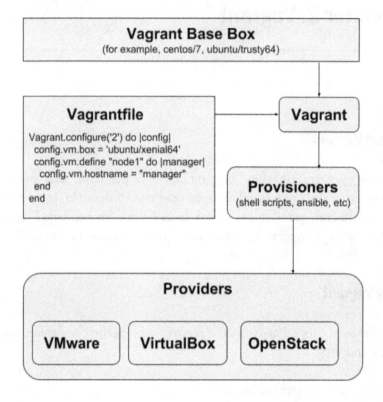

Vagrant main components:

Vagrant software

- Automates virtual machine build and configuration
- Has CLI using the "**vagrant**" utility available for these Operating Systems

Box

- Tar file that contains a virtual machine image
- Box files and their contained images are specific to each provider

Provider

- Interface which allows vagrant to communicate with different virtualization platforms
- By default it uses Oracle VirtualBox
- libvirt/KVM/OpenStack/etc provider are also available

Vagrantfile

- Plain text file that contains the instructions how to create virtual machine/machines
- Instructions are written using Ruby syntax

Installing Vagrant

Vagrant packages are available at https://www.vagrantup.com/ downloads. html.

Download the package for your OS and then simply install it. This is not it though. As we previously mentioned, Vagrant requires virtualization platform like Vmware, KVM, VirtualBox, AWS, Hyper-V or Docker.

MacOS X

- Download latest Vagrant software from the link above and install it
- Download and install VirtualBox from https://www.virtualbox. org/wiki/Downloads

CentOS

- Download latest Vagrant software from the link above and install it
- Install libvirt drivers and kvm

```
yum install epel-release -y
yum localinstall \
https://releases.hashicorp.com/vagrant/1.9.5/
vagrant  1.9.5  x86  64.rpm
```

```
yum install qemu libvirt libvirt-devel ruby-devel
gcc qemu-kvm
vagrant plugin install vagrant-libvirt
```

Ubuntu

```
apt install vagrant -y
```

Easy way to verify your vagrant is installed is to check Vagrant software version:

```
$ vagrant --version
Vagrant 1.9.5
```

Configuring Vagrant

Vagrant is easy to configure, and there are several ways of going it:

1. Via 'vagrant init' command, which generates Vagrantfile automatically

```
$ vagrant init <image _name>
```

2. Manually creating and editing Vagrantfile

```
$ nano Vagrantfile
Vagrant.configure("2") do |<node _name>|
  config.vm.box = "<image _path>"
end
```

For more images and browse through vagrant official repo following the next link https://app.vagrantup.com/boxes/search. Click on the image and you will be able to find two tabs: "Vagrantfile" and "New". They contain both options to configure your vagrant VM.

This is all for single VM provisioning, but what if you need multiple VMs. For that option you will have to manually create and edit Vagrantfile.

For multiple VMs

```
Vagrant.configure(2) do |config|
  config.vm.define "<node1>" do |<node1 _config>|
   <node1 _config>.vm.box = "<image _path>"
  end
  config.vm.define "<node2>" do |<node2 _config>|
   <node2 _config>.vm.box = "image _path"
  end
  config.vm.define "<node3>" do |<node3 _config>|
   <node2 _config>.vm.box = "image _path"
  end
end
```

For more information follow the link https://www.vagrantup.com/docs/multi-machine.

1. Via 'vagrant init' command

```
$ vagrant init centos/7
```

2. Manually creating and editing Vagrantfile

Configuration for 1 VM

```
Vagrant.configure("2") do |node1|
  config.vm.box = "centos/7"
end
```

Configuration for 2 VM

```
Vagrant.configure(2) do |config|
  config.vm.define "node1" do |node1|
   node1.vm.box = "centos/7"
  end
  config.vm.define "node2" do |node2|
   node2.vm.box = "ubuntu/xenial64"
```

```
    end
end
```

Managing Vagrant machines

Explanation

It is time to bring our first lab environment up. But before that, let's go through main Vagrant CLI commands you are going to use in this book:

Command	Description
vagrant up	Deploys VMs describe in Vagrantfile
vagrant halt	Destroys VMs described in Vagrantfile
vagrant halt	Stops the VM
vagrant reload	Restarts VM, loads new Vagrantfile configuration
vagrant resume	Resumes a suspended VM
vagrant ssh	Connects to VM via SSH
vagrant ssh-config	Shows running VMs configuration
vagrant global-status	Prints Vagrant status for this user (all VMs running)

For more options and detailed information use "help" subcommand:

```
$ vagrant help
Usage: vagrant [options] <command> [<args>]

    -v, --version    Print the version and exit.
    -h, --help       Print this help.

Common commands:
    box              manages boxes: installation,
removal, etc.
    destroy          stops and deletes all traces of
the vagrant machine
```

```
      global-status    outputs status Vagrant
environments for this user
      halt             stops the vagrant machine
      help             shows the help for a
subcommand
      init             initializes a new Vagrant
environment by creating a Vagrantfile
...
output truncated for brevity
...
`vagrant list-commands`.

$ vagrant box help
Usage: vagrant box <subcommand> [<args>]

Available subcommands:
      add
      list
      outdated
      prune
      remove
      repackage
      update
```

We are going to use following Vagrantfile that describes two VMs:

```
$ nano Vagrantfile

Vagrant.configure(2) do |config|
  config.vm.define "node1" do |node1|
   node1.vm.box = "centos/7"
  end
  config.vm.define "node2" do |node2|
   node2.vm.box = "ubuntu/xenial64"
  end
end
```

Bring up VMs

```
$ vagrant   up

Bringing machine 'default' up with 'virtualbox'
provider...
==> default: Importing base box 'centos/7'...
...
output truncated for brevity
...
==> default: Machine booted and ready!
...
output truncated for brevity
...
```

Check VMs status

```
$ vagrant status

Current machine states:

node1                      running (virtualbox)
node2                      running (virtualbox)

This environment represents multiple VMs. The VMs
are all listed
above with their current state. For more information
about a specific
VM, run `vagrant status NAME`.
```

Check VMs configuration for ssh

```
$ vagrant   ssh-config node1
Host node1
  HostName 127.0.0.1
  User vagrant
  Port 2200
  UserKnownHostsFile /dev/null
```

```
   StrictHostKeyChecking no
   PasswordAuthentication no
   IdentityFile /Users/dzuev/Downloads/Vagrant/.
vagrant/machines/node1/virtualbox/private_key
   IdentitiesOnly yes
   LogLevel FATAL

Host node2
   HostName 127.0.0.1
   User ubuntu
   Port 2201
   UserKnownHostsFile /dev/null
   StrictHostKeyChecking no
   PasswordAuthentication no
   IdentityFile /Users/dzuev/Downloads/Vagrant/.
vagrant/machines/node2/virtualbox/private_key
   IdentitiesOnly yes
   LogLevel FATAL
```

Login to vagrant VM and check your internet connectivity

```
$ vagrant ssh node1
[vagrant@localhost ~]$ ping 8.8.8.8 -c2
PING 8.8.8.8 (8.8.8.8) 56(84) bytes of data.
64 bytes from 8.8.8.8: icmp_seq=1 ttl=63
time=43.1 ms
64 bytes from 8.8.8.8: icmp_seq=2 ttl=63
time=46.5 ms

--- 8.8.8.8 ping statistics ---
2 packets transmitted, 2 received, 0% packet loss,
time 1002ms
```

It works! But before we start learning Ansible, make sure you know how to use other vagrant commands we mentioned previously.

If you want to rebuilding your VMs, that is pretty easy:

```
$ vagrant destroy
node2: Are you sure you want to destroy the 'node2'
VM? [y/N] y
==> node2: Forcing shutdown of VM...
==> node2: Destroying VM and associated drives...
    node1: Are you sure you want to destroy the
'node1' VM? [y/N] y
==> node1: Forcing shutdown of VM...
==> node1: Destroying VM and associated drives...
$ vagrant up
Bringing machine 'node1' up with 'virtualbox'
provider...
Bringing machine 'node2' up with 'virtualbox'
provider...
==> node1: Importing base box 'centos/7'...
==> node1: Matching MAC address for NAT networking...
==> node1: Checking if box 'centos/7' is up to date...
==> node1: Setting the name of the VM:
Vagrant _node1 _1506386569582 _6811
==> node1: Fixed port collision for 22 => 2222. Now
on port 2200.
==> node1: Clearing any previously set network
interfaces...
==> node1: Preparing network interfaces based on
configuration...
...
output truncated for brevity
...
==> node2: Importing base box 'ubuntu/xenial64'...
==> node2: Matching MAC address for NAT networking...
==> node2: Checking if box 'ubuntu/xenial64' is up
to date...
==> node2: Setting the name of the VM:
Vagrant _node2 _1506386600854 _62801
==> node2: Fixed port collision for 22 => 2222. Now
on port 2201.
==> node2: Clearing any previously set network
interfaces...
```

```
==> node2: Preparing network interfaces based on
configuration...
...
output truncated for brevity
...
```

If you are done for today, then simply shut down your VMs, and once you are ready, you can bring these VMs back.

```
$ vagrant halt
==> node2: Attempting graceful shutdown of VM...
==> node1: Attempting graceful shutdown of VM...

$ vagrant up
Bringing machine 'node1' up with 'virtualbox'
provider...
Bringing machine 'node2' up with 'virtualbox'
provider...
==> node1: Checking if box 'centos/7' is up to date...
==> node1: Clearing any previously set forwarded
ports...
==> node1: Fixed port collision for 22 => 2222. Now
on port 2200.
==> node1: Clearing any previously set network
interfaces...
==> node1: Preparing network interfaces based on
configuration...
...
output truncated for brevity
...
==> node1: Rsyncing folder: /Users/dzuev/Downloads/
Vagrant/ => /vagrant
==> node1: Machine already provisioned. Run `vagrant
provision` or use the `--provision`
==> node1: flag to force provisioning. Provisioners
marked to run always will still run.
==> node2: Checking if box 'ubuntu/xenial64' is up
to date...
```

```
==> node2: Clearing any previously set forwarded
ports...
==> node2: Fixed port collision for 22 => 2222. Now
on port 2201.
==> node2: Clearing any previously set network
interfaces...
==> node2: Preparing network interfaces based on
configuration...
...
output truncated for brevity
...
```

If you want to change your running VM configuration and add something new, like port forwarding or adding another interface, then simply edit the Vagrantfile and reload VMs.

```
$ cat Vagrantfile

Vagrant.configure(2) do |config|
    config.vm.define "node1" do |node1|
        node1.vm.box = "centos/7"
        node1.vm.network "private _network", ip:
"192.168.1.11"
        node1.vm.network "forwarded _port", guest:
161, host: 1611, protocol: "udp"
        node1.vm.network "forwarded _port", guest:
12000, host: 12001, protocol: "udp"
        node1.vm.network "forwarded _port", guest:
80, host: 8081, protocol: "tcp"
    end
    config.vm.define "node2" do |node2|
        node2.vm.box = "centos/7"
        node2.vm.network "private _network", ip:
"192.168.1.12"
        node2.vm.network "forwarded _port", guest:
161, host: 1612, protocol: "udp"
        node2.vm.network "forwarded _port", guest:
12000, host: 12002, protocol: "udp"
```

```
            node2.vm.network "forwarded _port", guest:
80, host: 8082, protocol: "tcp"
    end
    config.vm.define "node3" do |node3|
        node3.vm.box = "centos/7"
        node3.vm.network "private _network", ip:
"192.168.1.13"
        node3.vm.network "forwarded _port", guest:
161, host: 1613, protocol: "udp"
        node3.vm.network "forwarded _port", guest:
514, host: 5143, protocol: "udp"
        node3.vm.network "forwarded _port", guest:
12000, host: 12003, protocol: "udp"
        node3.vm.network "forwarded _port", guest:
80, host: 8083, protocol: "tcp"
    end
end


$ vagrant reload
==> node1: Attempting graceful shutdown of VM...
==> node1: Checking if box 'centos/7' is up to
date...
…
output truncated for brevity
…
==> node1: Preparing network interfaces based on
configuration...
    node1: Adapter 1: nat
    node1: Adapter 2: hostonly
==> node1: Forwarding ports...
    node1: 161 (guest) => 1611 (host) (adapter 1)
    node1: 12000 (guest) => 12001 (host) (adapter 1)
    node1: 80 (guest) => 8081 (host) (adapter 1)
    node1: 22 (guest) => 2222 (host) (adapter 1)
…
output truncated for brevity
…
==> node2: Attempting graceful shutdown of VM...
```

```
...
output truncated for brevity
...
==> node2: Preparing network interfaces based on
configuration...
    node2: Adapter 1: nat
    node2: Adapter 2: hostonly
==> node2: Forwarding ports...
    node2: 161 (guest) => 1612 (host) (adapter 1)
    node2: 12000 (guest) => 12002 (host) (adapter 1)
    node2: 80 (guest) => 8082 (host) (adapter 1)
    node2: 22 (guest) => 2200 (host) (adapter 1)
...
output truncated for brevity
...
==> node3: Attempting graceful shutdown of VM...
...
output truncated for brevity
...
==> node3: Preparing network interfaces based on
configuration...
    node3: Adapter 1: nat
    node3: Adapter 2: hostonly
==> node3: Forwarding ports...
    node3: 161 (guest) => 1613 (host) (adapter 1)
    node3: 514 (guest) => 5143 (host) (adapter 1)
    node3: 12000 (guest) => 12003 (host) (adapter 1)
    node3: 80 (guest) => 8083 (host) (adapter 1)
    node3: 22 (guest) => 2201 (host) (adapter 1)
...
output truncated for brevity
...
```

Make sure you have your VM applications and services persistent so they
survive a reboot, .e.g with 'systemctl enable' command.

Chapter 3. Ansible

About Ansible

Ansible is a configuration management tool like Chef, Puppet and SaltStack. It allows to automation routine system administration tasks like cloud VM provisioning, server hardening, packages installation, services configuration, networking, storage, and helping to automate your day-to-day routine jobs.

Do not underestimate Ansible, it is a great automation tool with a lot of potential in the future.

Why Ansible

There are a few things to tell about Ansible:

- hundreds of thousands of downloads monthly, over twelve hundreds built in modules and countless number of custom modules.
- thousands of customers.
- 21,000+ stars & 6,800+ forks on GitHub
- 2500+ contributors (Making Ansible one of the largest open source projects communities)
- New contributors added every day
- World-wide meetups taking place every week
- Ansible Galaxy is an official ansible repo for ansible roles: over 10,000 Roles
- 400,000+ downloads a month

Besides, ansible is extremely easy to use and it is written primarily in python, one of the most popular programming languages these days. So If you know python, you will be able to get most out of Ansible.

Ansible

Ansible architecture diagram and workflow

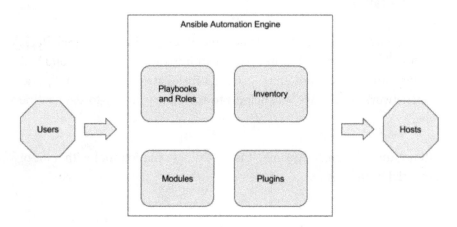

Ansible architecture is quite simple. At the very high level we have 3 main components:

- Ansible Users - actual users communicating with Ansible Engine.
- Ansible Engine – automation product which has several components involved.
- End hosts _ hosts under ansible control.

Ansible engine consists of:

- Playbooks and Roles – Ansible users write and interact with playbooks and roles written in primarily using YAML and Junja2.
- Modules – the heart of Ansible Engine. Currently over 1250 modules that executes automation tasks primarily written in python.
- Inventory – collection of end hosts and their properties.
- Plugins – different built-in and custom plugins types are available with Ansible, e.g. filters, vars, lookup, connection or test plugins.

Installing Ansible

Installing ansible is quite easy on both Linux or MacOS. The only prerequisite MacOS is to have brew installed. You can do that by following the link https://brew.sh/.

CentOS

```
$ yum install epel-release -y
$ yum install ansible -y
```

Fedora Linux

```
$ dnf install ansible -y
```

Ubuntu

```
$ apt install ansible -y
```

Mac OS X

```
$ brew install pip
$ pip install ansible
```

Check Ansible version

```
$ ansible --version
ansible 2.3.2.0
  config file = /etc/ansible/ansible.cfg
  configured module search path = Default w/o
overrides
  python version = 2.7.5 (default, Aug  4 2017,
00:39:18) [GCC 4.8.5 20150623 (Red Hat 4.8.5-16)]
```

Ansible commands

Ansible ships with a few commands which shortly explained in the table.

Command	Description
ansible	Runs a task on a single or multiple hosts
ansible-playbook	Runs playbooks
ansible-doc	Shows documentation on Ansible modules
ansible-vault	Manages encrypted files
ansible-galaxy	Manages roles using galaxy.ansible.com
ansible-pull	Runs playbooks from VCS server
ansible-console	A REPL for ad-hoc ansible tasks

We are going to work with most of these commands later in this chapter.

Setup your lab environment

Before we start, make sure you have you virtual environment up and running by pulling the source code

Below is your lab diagram:

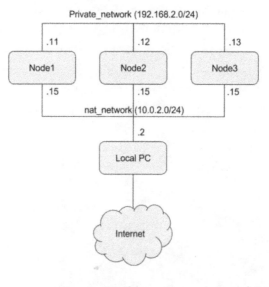

You should be also able to get all the necessary files from our git repo:

```
$ git clone https://github.com/flashdumper/
ansible _book.git
$ cd ansible _book/chapter _3/
setup _your _environment/
$ ls -l

total 120
-rw-r--r--@ 1 dzuev    staff      480 Sep 25 21:10
Vagrantfile
-rw-r--r--@ 1 dzuev    staff       40 Sep 25 21:24
ansible.cfg
-rw-r--r--@ 1 dzuev    staff       24 Sep 25 21:26 hosts
```

Below is the content of the ansible.cfg, hosts, and Vagrantfile.

```
$ cat ansible.cfg
[defaults]
inventory            = hosts

$ cat Vagrantfile
Vagrant.configure(2) do |config|
    config.vm.define "node1" do |node1|
        node1.vm.box = "centos/7"
        node1.vm.network "private _network", ip:
"192.168.2.11"
    end
    config.vm.define "node2" do |node2|
        node2.vm.box = "centos/7"
        node2.vm.network "private _network", ip:
"192.168.2.12"
    end
    config.vm.define "node3" do |node3|
        node3.vm.box = "ubuntu/xenial64"
        node3.vm.network "private _network", ip:
"192.168.2.13"
```

```
      end
end

$ cat hosts
[all]
node1
node2
node3
```

Bring your environment up and verify that it works

```
$ vagrant up
Bringing machine 'node1' up with 'virtualbox'
provider...
Bringing machine 'node2' up with 'virtualbox'
provider...
==> node1: Importing base box 'centos/7'...
==> node1: Matching MAC address for NAT networking...
==> node1: Checking if box 'centos/7' is up to date...
==> node1: Setting the name of the VM:
Vagrant_node1_1506386569582_6811
==> node1: Fixed port collision for 22 => 2202. Now
on port 2202.
==> node1: Clearing any previously set network
interfaces...
==> node1: Preparing network interfaces based on
configuration...
...
output truncated for brevity
...
==> node3: Importing base box 'ubuntu/xenial64'...
==> node3: Matching MAC address for NAT networking...
==> node3: Checking if box 'ubuntu/xenial64' is up
to date...
==> node3: Setting the name of the VM:
Vagrant_node2_1506386600854_62801
==> node3: Fixed port collision for 22 => 2204. Now
on port 2204.
```

```
==> node3: Clearing any previously set network
interfaces...
==> node3: Preparing network interfaces based on
configuration...
...
output truncated for brevity
...


$ vagrant ssh-config > ~/.ssh/config

$ vagrant status
Current machine states:

node1                      running (virtualbox)
node2                      running (virtualbox)
node3                      running (virtualbox)
```

This environment represents multiple VMs. The VMs are all listed above with their current state. For more information about a specific VM, run `vagrant status NAME`.

```
$ for i in {1..3}; do ssh node$i uptime; done
 05:43:42 up  2:26,  0 users,  load average: 0.00,
0.01, 0.05
 05:43:42 up  2:25,  0 users,  load average: 0.16,
0.05, 0.06
 05:43:31 up  2:24,  0 users,  load average: 0.00,
0.00, 0.00
```

Now you should be ready and good to go.

Ansible Components

Ansible is an agentless tool. On a client side (Linux) only thing that you need is ssh and python to be installed in order to be managed by Ansible. If you want to manage other than Linux devices, please check official Ansible website, On server side you need Ansible software and python.

File and Directory Structure

Ansible has very strict files and directory structure by default. You have to follow it in order for Ansible to work properly.

Here is how Ansible directories and files structure may look like:

```
|-- first _playbook.yml
|-- ansible.cfg
`-- hosts
```

Looks easy. Of course, It will get a bit complicated as we go, but let's take baby steps.

Let's take a look at another example below:

```
|-- ansible.cfg
|-- files
|    `-- file1.txt
|-- group _vars
|    `-- servers
|-- host _vars
|    |-- server1
|    `-- server2
|-- hosts
|-- library
|    `-- custom _module.sh
|-- playbooks
|    `-- sample _playbook.yml
|-- roles
|    `-- sample _role
|         |-- README.md
|         |-- defaults
|         |    `-- main.yml
|         |-- files
```

```
|          |-- handlers
|          |    `-- main.yml
|          |-- meta
|          |    `-- main.yml
|          |-- tasks
|          |    `-- main.yml
|          |-- templates
|          |-- tests
|          |    |-- inventory
|          |    `-- test.yml
|          `-- vars
|               `-- main.yml
`-- scripts
```

This is just to give you an idea. We are going to take a closer look at these files and directories one by one as we go through this book.

Configuration file

Ansible looks for ansible.cfg file in the order how they specified. The first found path is used:

- The ANSIBLE_CONFIG environment variable's location
- $PWD/ansible.cfg (current directory)
- ~/.ansible.cfg (home directory)
- /etc/ansible/ansible.cfg

Configuration file is an INI-format file which is divided into different sections. Below is minimum required parameters for you to start working with Ansible:

```
$ nano ansible.cfg

[defaults]
inventory           = hosts
```

The most important section is defaults. It specifies all the settings Ansible is going to use for while executing Ansible playbooks. In our case we specify just one option the inventory. This option specifies a file or directory used to get your managed hosts information from. Can be either an absolute or relative path e.g. inventory=inventory/, inventory=/etc/ansible/inventory, etc. That basically means you can specify either a file or directory.

For all other options please refer to the Ansible website: http://docs.ansible.com/ansible/latest/intro_inventory.html

Ansible inventory

A host inventory defines which hosts Ansible manages. Hosts may belong to groups which are typically used to identify the hosts' role in the datacenter. A host can be a member of more than one group.

There are ways in which host inventories can be defined:

- static host inventory may be defined by a text file
- an inventory path may be a directory
- dynamic host inventory may be generated from outside providers

Sample inventory file has INI-format file and can look like:

```
[mail_servers]
mail.example.com

[loadbalancer_servers]
lb1.example.com ansible_user=centos \
ansible_ssh_pass=STRONGPASS
lb2.example.com ansible_ssh_port=5309

[web_servers:children]
frontend_servers
backend_servers

[web_servers:vars]
site_root_dir = /var/www/html
```

```
[frontend _servers]
frontend[01:10].example.com

[backend _servers]
backend[a:f].example.com ansible _user=debian

[db _servers] db1.example.com ansible _user=oracle
```

Sections [mail_servers], [loadbalancer_servers], [frontend_servers], [backend_servers] and [db_servers] define the groups of hosts with the same names (without square brackets). There is no limitation on how many host records could be in a group and groups. Host entries might be defined in several ways:

- Directly specifying a hostname
- Using a range of hostnames with simple regex variables

These hostnames must be DNS resolvable. We use /etc/hosts file in the example below:

```
192.168.0.1 lb1.example.com lb1
192.168.0.2 lb2.example.com lb2
```

Section [web_servers:children] includes only other groups and cannot have host names. So in the example, the web_servers group includes next servers:

- frontend[01:10].example.com (10 servers, from frontend01.example.com … frontend10.example.com)
- backend[a:f].example.com ansible_user=debian (6 servers, from backenda.example.com to backendf.example.com)

Section [web_servers:vars] defines variables for that specific group of hosts. This variable is defined only for the group and is not available for other groups and hosts are not included in that group. This section does not create a new group so the group web_servers must be defined as well.

ansible_user and ansible_ssh_pass variables set the username and password for specified hosts or a group of hosts. These variables also might be defined for the all hosts of group if put them in the [...:vars] group, the variable site_root_dir is available for all hosts in the web_servers group.

There is a special group of hosts called [all]. This group includes all hosts defined in inventory. To define variables which are available for all hosts, the [all:vars] section might be used.

Modules

Ansible uses modules to perform any action against managed devices. Ansible comes with a lot of built-in modules, version 2.4 has over 1250 ones. Best way to explore these modules, is either using official ansible website or with the help of ansible-doc command.

Ansible documentation

You can get Ansible modules list, its options along with various example by following the link http://docs.ansible.com/ansible/latest/list_of_all_modules.html.

Helpful information about modules is available on the page http://docs.ansible.com/ansible/latest/modules_by_category.html. Those information is given for using in playbooks, which will be seen later.

```
$ ansible-doc -l
a10_server           Manage A10 Networks AX/SoftAX/
Thunder/vThunder devices' server object.
a10_server_axapi3   Manage A10 Networks AX/SoftAX/
Thunder/vThunder devices
a10_service_group   Manage A10 Networks AX/SoftAX/
Thunder/vThunder devices' service groups.
a10_virtual_server  Manage A10 Networks AX/SoftAX/
Thunder/vThunder devices' virtual servers.
accelerate           Enable accelerated mode on
remote node
```

```
acl                 Sets and retrieves file ACL
information.
add _host              add a host (and alternatively a
group) to the ansible-playbook in-memory inventory
...
output truncated for brevity
...
```

That's best and easiest way to look for a specific module. Use "grep" to make it even more efficient, e.g.

```
$ ansible-doc -l | grep junos
junos _command      Run arbitrary commands on an
Juniper JUNOS device
junos _config      Manage configuration on devices
running Juniper JUNOS
junos _facts       Collect facts from remote devices
running Juniper Junos
junos _netconf     Configures the Junos Netconf
system service
junos _package     Installs packages on remote
devices running Junos
junos _rpc         Runs an arbitrary RPC over
NetConf on an Juniper JUNOS device
junos _template    Manage configuration on remote
devices running Juniper JUNOS
junos _user        Manage local user accounts on
Juniper JUNOS devices
```

To check Ansible module specific information just specify Ansible module name with ansible-doc:

```
$ ansible-doc ping
> PING    (/usr/lib/python2.7/site-packages/ansible/
modules/system/ping.py)

  A trivial test module, this module always returns
`pong' on successful contact. It does not make
```

sense in playbooks, but it is useful from `/usr/bin/ansible'
   to verify the ability to login and that a usable python is configured. This is NOT ICMP ping, this is just a trivial test module.

EXAMPLES:
Test we can logon to 'webservers' and execute python with json lib.
ansible webservers -m ping

MAINTAINERS: Ansible Core Team, Michael DeHaan

METADATA:
        Status: ['stableinterface']
        Supported __by: core

To get a simple configuration snippet use ansible-doc -s option

```
$ ansible-doc -s hostname
- name: Manage hostname
  action: hostname
      name=                          # Name of the host
```

These modules can be used either using ad-hoc commands or in playbooks or roles. We will discuss both options in both later in this chapter.

Ad-Hoc commands

Make sure you have your virtual environment ready:

```
$ cd ../adhoc __commands/
$ vagrant up
$ vagrant ssh-config > ~/.ssh/config
```

Run simple verification command to make sure you able to connect to VMs:

```
$ for i in {1..3}; do ssh node$i uptime; done
```

```
17:15:39 up 4 min,   0 users,   load average: 0.01,
0.06, 0.04
17:15:39 up 3 min,   0 users,   load average: 0.03,
0.08, 0.05
17:15:38 up 1 min,   0 users,   load average: 0.40,
0.17, 0.06
```

Now we are ready to use Ansible commands. In the example below we are going to use ping module. It verifies connectivity to VMs via ssh and makes sure that proper python modules are installed. We are going to use this command often will to check connectivity to managed hosts.

```
$ ansible -m ping node1
node1 | SUCCESS => {
    "changed": false,
    "ping": "pong"
}
```

The syntax this command is simple, -m argument followed by a module name and last argument is a host/group. Another example is given below.

```
$ ansible -m ping all --limit 'group1:!node3'
node1 | SUCCESS => {
    "changed": false,
    "failed": false,
    "ping": "pong"
}
node2 | SUCCESS => {
    "changed": false,
    "failed": false,
    "ping": "pong"
}
```

Same effect but different approach. What the command does, it says "run ping module over all the hosts in the inventory file, limit to group1 and exclude node3".

Take a look at another example of Ansible copy module.

```
$ ansible -m copy -a 'dest=/tmp/test.txt
content="Made by Ansible."' node1
node1 | SUCCESS => {
    "changed": false,
    "checksum":
"1fab8a24c97a43be20e7b9e2f60e874e5b614be4",
    "dest": "/tmp/test.txt",
    "gid": 1001,
    "group": "users",
    "mode": "0644",
    "owner": "dm00",
    "path": "/tmp/test.txt",
    "size": 16,
    "state": "file",
    "uid": 1001
}

$ ssh node1 "cat /tmp/test.txt"
Made by Ansible.
```

The command above creates the /tmp/test.txt file with 'Made by Ansible' content on the node1 host. You can also go through the ansible-doc copy information and find other things it can do, such as:

- Making a backup copy
- Setting permissions
- Copying a file from a control host to remote hosts

Some modules have mandatory arguments that must be provided. You will be able to find those at http://docs.ansible.com/.

Now try to use file module and delete the file:

```
$ ansible -m file -a 'path=/tmp/test.txt state=absent'
node1
node1 | SUCCESS => {
```

```
    "changed": true,
    "failed": false,
    "path": "/tmp/test.txt",
    "state": "absent"
}

$ ssh node1 "cat /tmp/test.txt"
cat: /tmp/test.txt: No such file or directory
```

Take a look at another example. We are going to install the nginx package using the yum module by providing two arguments which accepted by the module:

- name=nginx
- state=installed

```
$ ansible -m yum -a 'name=nginx state=installed'
node1
node1 | FAILED! => {
    "changed": false,
    "failed": true,
    "msg": "No package matching 'nginx' found
available, installed or updated",
    "rc": 126,
    "results": [
        "No package matching 'nginx' found
available, installed or updated"
    ]
}
```

The output shows that task has FAILED, with human readable error message. In order to fix it, we have to install epel-release package first.

```
$ ansible -m yum -a 'name=epel-release
state=installed' node1
node1 | FAILED! => {
    "changed": false,
    "failed": true,
```

```
    "msg": "You need to be root to perform this
command.\n",
    "rc": 1,
    "results": [
        "Loaded plugins: fastestmirror\n"
    ]
}
```

We forgot to specify to use root credentials. Ansible-doc says to use –become/-b option

```
$ ansible --help | grep -A 1 'become '
    -b, --become          run operations with become
(does not imply password prompting)
```

Next command is going to fix it.

```
ansible -m yum -a 'name=epel-release
state=installed' -b node1
node1 | SUCCESS => {
    "changed": true,
    "failed": false,
    "msg": "warning: /var/cache/yum/x86_64/7/extras/
packages/epel-release-7-9.noarch.rpm:
...
output truncated for brevity
...
Complete!\n"
    ]
}
```

It worked without any errors. The output is not easy to read. Reason being is that is because the output is taken from CLI stdout console.

```
$ ansible -m yum -a 'name=nginx
state=installed' --become node1
node1 | SUCCESS => {
    "changed": true,
```

48

```
    "failed": false,
    "msg": "warning: /var/cache/yum/x86_64/7/extras/
packages/epel-release-7-9.noarch.rpm: Header V3 RSA/
SHA256 Signature, key ID
...
output truncated for brevity
...
Complete!\n"
    ]
}
```

Running modules using CLI is a simple way using Ansible, but it doesn't provide much flexibility and control of performed actions. Another ways of using Ansible is organizing required actions in playbooks.

Bring down your VMs and get ready for the new lab

```
$ vagrant destroy --force
$ cd ../playbooks/
$ vagrant up
$ vagrant ssh-config > ~/.ssh/config
```

Playbooks

Ansible playbook is a way to combine Ansible tasks in one place. A task is an operation Ansible performs. In other words an Ansible ad-hoc command = task.

Before you start using Ansible playbook, make sure that Ansible is able to connect to VM and run a task with an ad-hoc command.

```
$ ansible -m ping node1.example.com
node1.example.com | SUCCESS => {
    "changed": false,
    "ping": "pong"
}
```

```
$ ansible -m command -a "hostname" node1.example.com
node1.example.com | SUCCESS | rc=0 >>
localhost.localdomain
```

Each playbook is a separate file but playbooks may also include other playbooks. Create the playbook1.yml file in playbooks directory with following content:

```
$ cat solutions/playbook1.yml
---
- hosts: node1.example.com
  become: true
  gather_facts: false
  tasks:

  - name: Set a correct hostname
    hostname: name='node1.example.com'
```

To run this playbook, run following command:

```
$ ansible-playbook solutions/playbook1.yml

PLAY [node1.example.com]
******************************************************

TASK [Set a correct hostname]
******************************************************
changed: [node1.example.com]

PLAY RECAP
******************************************************
node1.example.com            :
ok=1     changed=1    unreachable=0     failed=0
```

Note that TASK "Set a correct hostname" is changed.

Verify the changes:

```
$ ansible -m command -a "hostname" node1.example.com

node1.example.com | SUCCESS | rc=0 >>
node1.example.com
```

Couple of things to note:

- Playbooks files may have any names and extensions
- A good practice is to collect all playbooks in one directory to keep the root directory more readable
- Playbooks are written using YAML markup language.

To learn more about YAML use the following this page http://docs.ansible.com/ansible/latest/YAMLSyntax.html. In short, YAML is a combination of lists and dictionaries. To learn more about lists and dictionaries use the following links:

- https://www.tutorialspoint.com/python/python_lists.htm
- https://www.tutorialspoint.com/python/python_dictionary.htm

The playbook starts with '---'. It Specifies the beginning of YAML formatted files and followed by 'hosts' section. This section defines the list of managed hosts. It may include group of hosts defined in inventory file or directly hosts without groups. You can also specify several hosts or groups. Another part of this section is 'become' key, you are familiar with it from ad-hoc part. It specifies whether you want to use root privileges or not. Ansible is pretty smart to figure out YAML format so you can omit '---' line at the beginning.

The example above also includes one more part called 'gathering facts'. By default, the variable gathers_facts is set to false. What it does is self explanatory, It takes all the properties of managed host like CPU, RAM, memory, hostames, IP addressing and other OS and hardware related information and sends back to control host for further processing. It takes time and additional resources to get these facts, so it is a good idea to turn it off if you are not using them:

```
gather _facts: no
```

You probably noticed that sometime we use variable value as "true/false", and sometimes it is "yes/no". They are all interchangeable. So there is no difference between 'yes' and 'true', as well as 'no' and 'false', so you can use one or the other method at your will.

The following is "tasks" section. This section consists of a list of tasks which we run on the managed hosts specified in the hosts section. The tasks are run in the order as they written in a playbook. Remember that tasks section is a list of dictionaries, that is why every task is separated by the dash letter '-'.

It is important to follow YAML syntax and indentation. Check a sample playbook structure:

```
- hosts: <host(s)>
  become: yes
  gather _facts: no
  tasks:
  - module: arg1=value1 arg2=value2 …
  - module: arg1=value1 arg2=value2 …
...
```

It takes time to get used to it, but once you play with YAML for a while, you have no problems at all.

Let's copy the playbook1.yml to playbook2.yml and add into the new playbook a new task:

```
$ cat solutions/playbook2.yml
- hosts: node1.example.com
  become: yes
  gather _facts: no
  tasks:

  - name: Set a correct hostname
    hostname: name='node1.example.com'
```

```
- name: Create the /tmp/test.txt file
  become: no
  copy:
      content: |
          This file is made by an Ansible playbook.
      dest: /tmp/test.txt
```

In this new playbook we added another task. Take a look at the structure carefully and check if you have any questions regarding the structure. It is not easy to understand if you see it for the first time. All tasks have the same indentation level since they are in the same list. Then we have the 'become' statement and the 'copy' section. The 'copy' module has its properties, in our case these are 'content' and 'dest'. That is the main reason for them to be in a different indentation level. Do not worry, you will get used to YAML structure with time.

Now run this new playbook:

```
$ ansible-playbook solutions/playbook2.yml

PLAY [node1.example.com]
*********************************************************

TASK [Set a correct hostname]
*********************************************************
ok: [node1.example.com]

TASK [Create the /tmp/test.txt file]
*********************************************************
changed: [node1.example.com]

PLAY RECAP
*********************************************************
node1.example.com           :
ok=2    changed=1    unreachable=0    failed=0
```

Note that you see that one of the TASKS has 'changed' status and all the other ones are in 'ok' status. That is because we took playbook1.yml and added a new task. And since there was nothing to change for the first task, Ansible just created a new file 'text.txt' and let us know about the change.

Now take a look at the playbook3.yml.

```
$ cat solutions/playbook3.yml
- include: playbook1.yml
- import __playbook: playbook2.yml
```

Few things to pay attention to, here:

The "include" statement is the same as "import_playbook". Ansible is still going through a lot of transformation and development and one commands are getting replaced with the others. You can use the 'include' module, but it is going to be deprecated in the future.

This new playbook3.yml just calls other 2 playbooks. Depending on your environments and tasks you might want to use this method. There are several methods of calling your playbooks as well. Take a look at the examples below:

```
$ ansible-playbook solutions/playbook1.yml solutions/
playbook2.yml

PLAY [node1.example.com]
*************************************************************
*************************************************

TASK [Set a correct hostname]
*************************************************************
*******************************************
ok: [node1.example.com]

PLAY RECAP
*************************************************************
*************************************************************
****
node1.example.com          :
ok=1     changed=0     unreachable=0     failed=0
```

```
PLAY [node1.example.com]
************************************************************
*************************************************

TASK [Set a correct hostname]
************************************************************
******************************************
ok: [node1.example.com]

TASK [Create the /tmp/test.txt file]
************************************************************
***********************************
ok: [node1.example.com]

PLAY RECAP
************************************************************
************************************************************
****
node1.example.com              :
ok=3     changed=0     unreachable=0     failed=0


$ ansible-playbook solutions/playbook3.yml


[DEPRECATION WARNING]: 'include' for playbook
includes. You should use 'import_playbook' instead.
This feature will be removed in version 2.8.
Deprecation warnings can be disabled by setting
deprecation_warnings=False in ansible.cfg.
PLAY [node1.example.com]
************************************************************
*********************************************

TASK [Set a correct hostname]
************************************************************
******************************************
ok: [node1.example.com]
```

```
PLAY [node1.example.com]
****************************************************
************************************************

TASK [Set a correct hostname]
****************************************************
******************************************
ok: [node1.example.com]

TASK [Create the /tmp/test.txt file]
****************************************************
***********************************
ok: [node1.example.com]

PLAY RECAP
****************************************************
****************************************************
****

node1.example.com               :
ok=3    changed=0    unreachable=0    failed=0
```

Same result, different approach. Choose whichever method you like the most.

There is a very useful ad-hoc command that shows you the tasks defined in your playbook. Run this command to see a list of tasks defined in a playbook.

```
$ ansible-playbook solutions/playbook3.
yml --list-tasks
```

```
[DEPRECATION WARNING]: 'include' for playbook
includes. You should use 'import_playbook' instead.
This feature will be removed
in version 2.8. Deprecation warnings can be
disabled by setting deprecation_warnings=False in
ansible.cfg.
```

```
playbook: playbook3.yml

   play #1 (node1.example.com): node1.example.com
TAGS: []
     tasks:
       Set a correct hostname TAGS: []

   play #2 (node1.example.com): node1.example.com
TAGS: []
     tasks:
       Set a correct hostname TAGS: []
       Create the /tmp/test.txt file TAGS: []
```

Another good thing is to check playbook syntax in order to make sure it runs without any errors:

```
$ ansible-playbook solutions/playbook1.yml solutions/
playbook2.yml --syntax-check

playbook: playbook1.yml

playbook: playbook2.yml
```

Bring down current lab and get ready for a new one.

```
$ vagrant destroy --force
$ cd ../variables/
$ vagrant up
$ vagrant ssh-config > ~/.ssh/config
```

Variables

Like any other programming language Ansible supports variables. The power of variables must not be underestimated. Variables can help to simplify your Ansible project and increase usability.

Variables provide a very convenient way to manage dynamic values for a given environment in your Ansible project. Some examples of values that variables might contain, include:

- List of users to create
- List of Packages to install on the systems
- Services to restart
- Files to remove
- Archives to retrieve from the Internet
- IP addresses

Names of variables might consist of upper and lowercase letters, numbers and underscores. A variable cannot begin with a digit and include whitespaces. Variables should not conflict with Ansible key words. Examples of the correct variables' names are:

- var1
- _VAR
- another_variable
- _3var
- _2017_date

Examples of the incorrect variables names are:

- 1var - starts from a digit
- @var1 – reserved special character used
- var – reserved key word used

Variables are loaded from multiple places when Ansible runs:

- ansible.cfg – limited number of variables that might redefined later
- Ad-hoc commands
- Inventory
- Host variables
- Group variables
- Playbooks
- Roles
- Included files

We are going to explain this in the following sections of this book. To simplify the understanding just need to know that the variables are used by three levels of a project:

- Global scope: any host, and any task access those variables.
- Play scope: variables are available in only playbooks they are defined in.
- Host scope: only a specific host has access to such variables.

The same variable might be defined more than one time. In such cases, need to follow to an order a variable is defined in:

- Variables provided in a command line have the highest priority
- Inventory variables
- Host variables
- Group variables
- Playbook variables
- Roles variables

If you need to have some default value of a variable, it might be defined at a lower level and then it may be redefined again at a higher level, if required. This is also a best practice and help avoiding errors in the future. Also keep your playbooks documented so other people do not need to read entire playbooks to understand which variables should be passed for successful launching.

Variables in inventory

Our inventory file should look like this:

```
$ cat inventory
[hostgroup-1]
node1.example.com ansible_ssh_port=2221
ansible_ssh_private_key_file='.vagrant/machines/
node1.example.com/virtualbox/private_key'

node2.example.com ansible_ssh_port=2222
ansible_ssh_private_key_file='.vagrant/machines/
node2.example.com/virtualbox/private_key'
```

```
[hostgroup-1:vars]
ansible _host = 127.0.0.1
ansible _user = vagrant
```

The variables in the inventory file are following right after hostnames, and their values follow after the equal '=' sign. E.g. 'ansible_user' is a variable and 'vagrant' is its value. Some of them are defined in the same line along with hostnames. These variables called Host Variables. Only the hosts which have variables defined this way recognize the variables as its own. Other hosts can also get access to other hosts' variables if necessary.

Another sort of variables that might be defined in inventory files are called Group Variables. Group Variables defined in a section with the same name as a group of hosts with the colon mark and the 'var' word after it. In the above example, the 'hostgroup-1:vars' defines the variables that available to each of the hosts in the hostgroup-1 host group. In that case the hosts node1.example.com and node2.example.com have the variables ansible_host=127.0.0.1, and ansible_user=vagrant available for each of them like if they would be defined individually.

If you need to have variables available for all groups defined in inventory, you need to create the section called 'all:vars' and specify global variables in there. This approach eliminates the need to specify the same data for each of groups or hosts.

Variables in playbooks

Playbook is another place for tasks, the actions that Ansible is being done when running. So in playbooks we can also define variables and use them in tasks. Take a look at the playbook1.yml file.

```
$ cat solutions/playbook1.yml
- hosts: node1.example.com
  become: yes
  vars:
    new _hostname: node1-new.example.com
  tasks:
```

```
- name: Set new hostname to node1
  hostname: name='{{ new _hostname }}'
```

Run this playbook:

```
$ ansible-playbook solutions/playbook1.yml

PLAY [node1.example.com]
*************************************************************
***********************************************

TASK [Gathering Facts]
*************************************************************
***************************************************
ok: [node1.example.com]

TASK [Set new hostname to the node1]
*************************************************************
**********************************
changed: [node1.example.com]

PLAY RECAP
*************************************************************
*************************************************************
****
node1.example.com          :
ok=2    changed=1    unreachable=0    failed=0
```

Verify the changes with ad-hoc command:

```
$ ansible -m command -a "hostname" node1.example.com
node1.example.com | SUCCESS | rc=0 >>
node1-new.example.com
```

In the playbook above we define the "new_hostname" variable, and this variable is being used in the following tasks. In the example, the task 'Set new hostname to the node1' uses this new_hostname variable. At the same time, all managed hosts also recognize the new_hostname variable as its own. This playbook is run only on the node1.example.com host, but if you would put there, for example, the group named 'all', then on the all hosts in the inventory would be changed hostname to the same value 'node1-new. example.com'.

In order to get a variable value, the variable is called in double curly brackets inside single quotes. This is a special construction that says to interpret the word inside as a variable. Variables like many other constructions in Ansible are handled by Jinja2 template engine http://jinja.pocoo.org/. Jinja2 is a very popular templating language widely used in other programming languages, tools, and applications.

Looking back, if we would define the same variable in the inventory file with other value, that new value would be used then. It becomes possible because the variables in the inventory file take precedence over variables in a playbook.

Take a look at other example playbook2.yml:

```
$ cat solutions/playbook2.yml
- hosts: all
  become: yes
  vars _files:
    - vars1.yml
  tasks:
  - name: Creating the devops account
    user:
      comment: '{{ devops _comment }}'
      createhome: '{{ devops _createhome }}'
      name: '{{ devops _login }}'
```

Run this playbook:

```
$ ansible-playbook solutions/playbook2.yml

PLAY [all]
*************************************************************
```

```
*************************************************************
****

TASK [Gathering Facts]
*************************************************************
**************************************************
ok: [node2.example.com]
ok: [node1.example.com]

TASK [Creating the devops account]
*************************************************************
**************************************
changed: [node1.example.com]
changed: [node2.example.com]

PLAY RECAP
*************************************************************
*************************************************************
****
node1.example.com          :
ok=2     changed=1     unreachable=0     failed=0
node2.example.com          :
ok=2     changed=1     unreachable=0     failed=0
```

And verify the changes with an ad-hoc command:

```
$ ansible -m command -a "id devops" all
node1.example.com | SUCCESS | rc=0 >>
uid=1001(devops) gid=1001(devops) groups=1001(devops)

node2.example.com | SUCCESS | rc=0 >>
uid=1001(devops) gid=1001(devops) groups=1001(devops)
```

In this example, we used "vars_files" section, which instructs Ansible to read variables from external file. The vars1.yml file is written on YAML language. Let's check what inside var1.yml file:

```
$ cat solutions/vars1.yml
devops_comment: Development Operations Account
devops_createhome: yes
devops_login: devops
```

The task 'Creating the devops account' in playbook2.yml uses variables defined inside the vars1.yml file like as they would be defined directly in the playbook2.yml file. There is no difference where to define variables, but for the best practice you'd better define variables in separate files so you can utilize them later or maybe in some other projects.

Ansible is shipped with the include_vars module. This module allows to load variables from external files the same way as it done by the vars instruction. And there is one more module that allows to define dynamic variables is set_fact. Read mode information by using the ansible-doc command. See the example playbook, playbook3.yml:

```
$ cat solutions/playbook3.yml
- hosts: all
  become: yes
  tasks:
  - name: Loading variables from external file
    include_vars: vars1.yml

  - name: Creating the devops account
    user:
      comment: '{{ devops_comment }}'
      createhome: '{{ devops_createhome }}'
      name: '{{ devops_login }}'

  - name: Define a dynamic variable
    set_fact:
      var1: This is a dynamic variable var1
      var2: This is a dynamic variable var2

  - name: Debug output of the var1
    debug: msg='{{ var1 }}'
```

```
- name: Debug output of the var2
  debug: msg='{{ var2 }}'
```

All of the examples above show that variables can be defined in multiple ways. Which way you chose usually depends on Ansible project scale. Or if you have too many variables, probably it is a good idea to place them in separate files so they can be used later by other playbooks. If you have a couple of variables, keeping them in playbook would also be a good thing to do.

Now run the playbook above:

```
$ ansible-playbook solutions/playbook3.yml
PLAY [all]
**************************************************************
**************************************************************
****

TASK [Gathering Facts]
**************************************************************
*************************************************
ok: [node2.example.com]
ok: [node1.example.com]

TASK [Loading variables from external file]
**************************************************************
***************************
ok: [node1.example.com]
ok: [node2.example.com]

TASK [Creating the devops account]
**************************************************************
**************************************
ok: [node1.example.com]
ok: [node2.example.com]

TASK [Define a dynamic variable]
**************************************************************
**************************************
```

```
ok: [node1.example.com]
ok: [node2.example.com]

TASK [Debug output of the var1]
*********************************************************
*****************************************
ok: [node1.example.com] => {
    "msg": "This is a dynamic variable var1"
}
ok: [node2.example.com] => {
    "msg": "This is a dynamic variable var1"
}

TASK [Debug output of the var2]
*********************************************************
*****************************************
ok: [node1.example.com] => {
    "msg": "This is a dynamic variable var2"
}
ok: [node2.example.com] => {
    "msg": "This is a dynamic variable var2"
}

PLAY RECAP
*********************************************************
*********************************************************
****
node1.example.com                 :
ok=6    changed=0    unreachable=0    failed=0
node2.example.com                 :
ok=6    changed=0    unreachable=0    failed=0
```

The debug module is very useful while troubleshooting Ansible, we use the debug module often in this book.

Bring down current lab and get ready for the new one.

```
$ vagrant destroy --force
$ cd ../tasks_control/
$ vagrant up
```

Tasks

In previous chapters, we learnt how to write playbooks. A playbook is a text and YAML formatted file with usually several sections included. The task section is a list of modules and their properties that actually do all the automation job. In this chapter, we will learn basic constructions of tasks and how to work with tasks.

As mentioned earlier, every task represents one module. If you need to run several modules just split them down by several tasks. Here is an example:

```
$ cat solutions/playbook1.yml
- hosts: node1.example.com
  become: yes
  tasks:
    - name: Update /etc/ssh/sshd_config file
      lineinfile:
        path: /etc/ssh/sshd_config
        regexp: '^PermitRootLogin.*$'
        line: 'PermitRootLogin yes'

    - name: Restart SSH service
      service: name=sshd state=restarted
```

Task control

So far, we used only modules and their arguments, and it is not always enough. Luckily Ansible is very flexible and we can extend tasks with special keywords which makes tasks more manageable.

Handlers

Ansible is designed to be idempotent and can notify other modules when a change has been made. It can be done with a help of **notify** statement of a task. If there is a change while executing a specific task, you can run another task specified in the **handlers** section. Usually people use handlers to restart a service when there is a change in the config but you can use handlers to trigger something else, like sending an email or execute another job.

Take a look at the example below:

```
$ cat solutions/playbook _handlers1.yml
- hosts: node1.example.com
  become: yes
  tasks:
    - name: Update /etc/ssh/sshd _config file
      lineinfile:
        path: /etc/ssh/sshd _config
        regexp: '^PermitRootLogin.*$'
        line: 'PermitRootLogin yes'
      notify:
        - Restart SSH service

  handlers:
    - name: Restart SSH service
      service: name=sshd state=restarted
```

Run the playbook above:

```
$ ansible-playbook solutions/playbook _handlers1.yml

PLAY [node1.example.com]
**********************************************************
*************************************************

TASK [Gathering Facts]
**********************************************************
```

```
**************************************************
ok: [node1.example.com]

TASK [Update /etc/ssh/sshd __config file]
**********************************************************
********************************
changed: [node1.example.com]

RUNNING HANDLER [Restart SSH service]
**********************************************************
*********************************
changed: [node1.example.com]

PLAY RECAP
**********************************************************
**********************************************************
****
node1.example.com            :
ok=3    changed=2    unreachable=0    failed=0
```

To simplify our efforts by enumerating all handlers in each task we can
attach to the needed handlers the **listen** option and give to it a common
name. In the tasks which should trigger executing those handlers we can
just refer to this listen name.

Take a look at the example below:

```
$ cat solutions/playbook __handlers2.yml

- hosts: node1.example.com
  become: yes
  tasks:
    - name: Install epel-release repository
      yum: name=epel-release state=installed

    - name: Install php-fpm, nginx, and mariadb
packages
      yum: name='{{ item }}' state=installed
```

```
    with __items:
    - php-fpm
    - nginx
    - mariadb-server
    notify:
    - Complete restarting of a website

  handlers:
    - name: Restart Web service
      service: name=nginx state=restarted
      listen: Complete restarting of a website

    - name: Restart PHP-FPM service
      service: name=php-fpm state=restarted
      listen: Complete restarting of a website

    - name: Restart Database
      service: name=mariadb state=restarted
      listen: Complete restarting of a website
```

The output should look like this:

```
$ ansible-playbook solutions/playbook __handlers2.yml

PLAY [node1.example.com]
*************************************************************
**************************************************
   
TASK [Gathering Facts]
*************************************************************
***********************************************
ok: [node1.example.com]

TASK [Install epel-release repository]
*************************************************************
******************************
changed: [node1.example.com]
```

```
TASK [Install php-fpm, nginx, and mariadb packages]
**********************************************************
********************
changed: [node1.example.com] => (item=[u'php-fpm',
u'nginx', u'mariadb-server'])

RUNNING HANDLER [Restart Web service]
**********************************************************
*********************************
changed: [node1.example.com]

RUNNING HANDLER [Restart PHP-FPM service]
**********************************************************
*****************************
changed: [node1.example.com]

RUNNING HANDLER [Restart Database]
**********************************************************
************************************
changed: [node1.example.com]

PLAY RECAP
**********************************************************
**********************************************************
****
node1.example.com             :
ok=6    changed=5    unreachable=0    failed=0
```

Few things to note here:

- Handlers names and the topics are available globally
- If two tasks have the same name, only one specified first will run
- Handlers are called in the order they defined in a playbook
- Handlers are called only if a task acquires the change state and the only those handlers which listed in that task

If you need to run a handler immediately upon registering a task state as changed, a special module should be used as shown in the example below.

Ansible has a module that called **meta** that may influence internal state or execution. Call this module after a task to do the trick.

Run the playbook below:

```
$ cat solutions/playbook_handlers3.yml
- hosts: node1.example.com
  become: yes
  tasks:
    - name: Update /etc/ssh/sshd_config file
      lineinfile:
        path: /etc/ssh/sshd_config
        regexp: '^PermitRootLogin.*$'
        line: 'PermitRootLogin no'
      notify:
        - Restart SSH service

    - meta: flush_handlers

    - name: Create user devops
      user: name=devops

  handlers:
    - name: Restart SSH service
      service: name=sshd state=restarted
```

You should see the output:

```
$ ansible-playbook solutions/playbook_handlers3.yml

PLAY [node1.example.com]
**********************************************************
*************************************************

TASK [Gathering Facts]
**********************************************************
*************************************************
ok: [node1.example.com]
```

```
TASK [Update /etc/ssh/sshd _config file]
*************************************************************
*******************************
changed: [node1.example.com]

RUNNING HANDLER [Restart SSH service]
*************************************************************
*********************************
changed: [node1.example.com]

TASK [Create user devops]
*************************************************************
***********************************************
changed: [node1.example.com]

PLAY RECAP
*************************************************************
*****************************************************
node1.example.com            :
ok=4     changed=3     unreachable=0     failed=0
```

Tags

In complex playbooks, you may require to run only some of them without running a whole playbook. Playbooks and tasks support tags.

Take a look at the example below:

```
$ cat solutions/playbook _tags1.yml

- hosts: node2.example.com
  become: yes
  tasks:
    - name: Install Apache
      yum: name=httpd state=installed
      tags:
      - install
```

73

```
    - name: Set server name
      lineinfile:
        path: /etc/httpd/conf/httpd.conf
        regexp: '^ServerName.*$'
        line: 'ServerName {{ inventory_hostname }}'
      tags:
      - configure


    - name: Restart Apache
      service: name=httpd state=restarted
enabled=true
      tags:
      - restart
```

Here we have three tasks, with each of them having different tags. A good way to specify all the task in the playbook is to specify 'list-tags' option:

```
$ ansible-playbook solutions/playbook_tags1.
yml --list-tags

playbook: playbook_tags1.yml

  play #1 (node2.example.com): node2.example.com
TAGS: []
      TASK TAGS: [configure, install, restart]
```

Now we can selectively run these tasks:

```
$ ansible-playbook solutions/playbook_tags1.
yml --tags install,configure

PLAY [node2.example.com]
************************************************************
**************************************************

TASK [Gathering Facts]
************************************************************
**************************************************
```

```
ok: [node2.example.com]

TASK [Install Apache]
*********************************************************
**************************************************
changed: [node2.example.com]

TASK [Set server name]
*********************************************************
***************************************************
changed: [node2.example.com]

PLAY RECAP
*********************************************************
*********************************************************
****
node2.example.com                :
ok=3    changed=2    unreachable=0    failed=0
```

or by skipping the tagged tasks:

```
$ ansible-playbook solutions/playbook __tags1.
yml --skip-tags configure

PLAY [node2.example.com]
*********************************************************
************************************************

TASK [Gathering Facts]
*********************************************************
**********************************************
ok: [node2.example.com]

TASK [Install Apache]
*********************************************************
***********************************************
ok: [node2.example.com]
```

```
TASK [Restart Apache]
*****************************************************************
****************************************************
changed: [node2.example.com]

PLAY RECAP
*****************************************************************
*****************************************************************
****
node2.example.com              :
ok=3     changed=1     unreachable=0     failed=0
```

The same tags might be used within multiple tasks, that would mean that all tasks which have that tag will be run. If you do not specify any tags, the whole playbook will run.

Instead of tagging tasks one by one, we can tag a whole playbook. This is useful when you run a few playbooks at once include playbooks within other playbooks.

We should be also able to see a default web page after running last playbook. Just open the URL http://localhost:8082/ in any browser or execute the curl command:

```
$ curl localhost:8082
<!DOCTYPE html PUBLIC "-//W3C//DTD XHTML 1.1//
EN" "http://www.w3.org/TR/xhtml11/DTD/xhtml11.
dtd"><html><head>
...
output truncated for brevity
...
</body></html>
```

Now let's take a look at the example below:

```
$ cat solutions/playbook __tags2.yml
```

```
- hosts: node2.example.com
  become: yes
  tags:
  - apache
  tasks:
    - name: Install Apache
      yum: name=httpd state=installed
      tags:
      - install

    - name: Set server name
      lineinfile:
        path: /etc/httpd/conf/httpd.conf
        regexp: '^ServerName.*$'
        line: 'ServerName {{ inventory_hostname }}'
      tags:
      - configure

    - name: Restart Apache
      service: name=httpd state=restarted
enabled=yes
      tags:
      - restart
```

Verify a list of the tags available in this playbook:

```
$ ansible-playbook solutions/playbook_tags2.
yml --list-tags

playbook: playbook_tags2.yml

  play #1 (node2.example.com): node2.example.com
TAGS: [apache]
      TASK TAGS: [apache, configure, install,
restart]
```

Note that we can have multiple tag hierarchies. The tag "apache" will run the whole playbook with all the tasks underneath, and we can also work with specific task tags. Let's take a look at the following example:

```
$ ansible-playbook solutions/playbook _tags2.
yml --tags apache --skip-tags configure

PLAY [node2.example.com]
**********************************************************
*************************************************

TASK [Gathering Facts]
**********************************************************
**************************************************
ok: [node2.example.com]

TASK [Install Apache]
**********************************************************
*************************************************
ok: [node2.example.com]

TASK [Restart Apache]
**********************************************************
**************************************************
changed: [node2.example.com]

PLAY RECAP
**********************************************************
**********************************************************
****
node2.example.com              :
ok=3    changed=1    unreachable=0    failed=0
```

Analyze the output and try to understand why we have this result.

For more examples check Ansible documentation via http://docs.ansible.com/ansible/playbooks_tags.html.

Conditions

Very often you have tasks which should or shouldn't run depending on a specific condition. You can use the 'when' statement to help with it. This statement works similar to other programming languages. A task is run only when a specified condition is met.

Take a look at the example below:

```
$ cat solutions/playbook_conditional1.yml

- hosts: all
  become: yes
  vars:
    users: user4
  tasks:
    - name: Create users on node1.example.com
      user: name='{{ users }}'
      when: inventory_hostname == 'node1.
example.com'
```

Run the playbook:

```
$ ansible-playbook solutions/
playbook_conditional1.yml

PLAY [all]
************************************************************
************************************************************
****

TASK [Gathering Facts]
************************************************************
*************************************************
ok: [node2.example.com]
ok: [node1.example.com]
```

```
TASK [Create users on node1.example.com]
*********************************************************
***************************
skipping: [node2.example.com]
changed: [node1.example.com]

PLAY RECAP
*********************************************************
*********************************************************
****
node1.example.com          :
ok=2      changed=1    unreachable=0    failed=0
node2.example.com          :
ok=1      changed=0    unreachable=0    failed=0
```

The **when** keyword is used on the same indentation level as the user module. It is also can be used within any task. In the example, the task is run only if 'inventory_hostname' variable has the 'node1.example.com' value. All managed hosts check if they meet this condition. Instead, if you need to test several conditions, they might be combined by using logical operators OR and AND, like shown in the example below.

```
$ cat solutions/playbook__conditional2.yaml

- hosts: all
  become: yes
  vars:
    users: user4
  tasks:
    - name: Create users on node1.example.com if its
OS is RedHat based
      user: name='{{ users }}'
      when: inventory_hostname == 'node1.example.
com' and ansible_os_family == 'RedHat'
```

You may notice that we used 'ansible_os_family' variable. It is not a built-in variable but rather something that comes after playing default task "Gathering Facts". We are going to discuss this later in the book.

The output should look like:

```
$ ansible-playbook solutions/
playbook __conditional2.yml

PLAY [all]
*************************************************************
*************************************************************
****

TASK [Gathering Facts]
*************************************************************
*******************************************************
ok: [node1.example.com]
ok: [node2.example.com]

TASK [Create users on node1.example.com if its OS is
RedHat based]
*************************************************************
*****
skipping: [node2.example.com]
ok: [node1.example.com]

PLAY RECAP
*************************************************************
*************************************************************
****
node1.example.com               :
ok=2    changed=0    unreachable=0    failed=0
node2.example.com               :
ok=1    changed=0    unreachable=0    failed=0
```

In this example, the task is run on the node1.example.com host. In the **when** statement, you may use next operators to check an expression result.

Operator	Example
Equal	"{{ max_memory }} == 512"
Less than	"{{ min_memory }} < 128"
Greater than	"{{ min_memory }} > 256"
Less than or equal to	"{{ min_memory }} <= 256"
Greater than or equal to	"{{ min_memory }} >= 512"
Not equal to	"{{ min_memory }} != 512"
Variable exists	"{{ min_memory }} is defined"
Variable does not exist	"{{ min_memory }} is not defined"
Variable is set to 1, True, or yes	"{{ available_memory }}"
Variable is set to 0, False, or no	"not {{ available_memory }}"
Value is present in a variable or an array	"{{ users }} in users["db_admins"]"

Find out below some examples:

```
when: inventory_hostname != "node1.example.com"
when: ansible_mem_total > 4096
when: inventory_hostname.split('.')[-2:] | join('.')
== "example.com"
when: ansible_cpu_count == 4
when: cluster_member | default(false)
when: 'user1' in ['user1', 'user2', 'user3']
when: var1 is defined and var1 > 10
```

In the examples above the 'when' statements can have different values: boolean values, expressions that evaluate to boolean, filters that return a boolean value, etc. Anything that returns a boolean result may be put in the when statement.

For more examples use the Ansible documentation via http://docs.ansible.com/ansible/latest/playbooks_conditionals.html

Loops

If you have multiple tasks of the same module but different values like installing a list of packages using the yum module, it is probably better to use the loops technique.

Below is an example without using loops.

```
- yum: name="wget"
- yum: name="git"
- yum: name="tcpdump"
```

Depending on the number of packages you are required to install, a list of repeatable tasks will vary but still that is not an effective approach. For simplifying our work we can use the 'with_items' statement instead.

Take a look at the example below:

```
$ cat solutions/playbook_loops1.yml
- hosts: node1.example.com
  become: yes
  tasks:
    - name: Installing packages
      yum: name='{{ item }}'
      with_items:
      - wget
      - git
      - tcpdump
      when: ansible_distribution == 'CentOS'
```

When the 'with_items' statement used, the 'item' variable becomes available. It basically replaces the items in 'with_items' statement on each iteration.

Check the output:

```
$ ansible-playbook solutions/playbook _loops1.yml
TASK [Gathering Facts]
*********************************************************
***************************************************
ok: [node1.example.com]

TASK [Installing packages]
*********************************************************
**********************************************
changed: [node1.example.com] => (item=[u'wget',
u'git', u'tcpdump'])

PLAY RECAP
*********************************************************
*********************************************************
****
node1.example.com          :
ok=2    changed=1    unreachable=0    failed=0
```

List of hashes

Sometimes we have more complex structures. In the example below we give you an example of using a list of variables with the 'with_items' statement.

```
$ cat solutions/playbook _loops2.yml
- hosts: node1.example.com
  become: yes
  tasks:
    - name: Creating accounts
      user:
        name: '{{ item.user }}'
        comment: '{{ item["comment"] }}'
        home: '{{ item.home }}'
      with _items:
      - { user: devops, comment: DevOps Account,
home: /home/devops }
      - { user: operator, comment: Operator Account,
home: /var/operator }
```

```
      - { user: techadm, comment: Technical
Support, home: /home/techadm }
```

If you familiar with Python or any other programming language, syntax should be easy for you to read and understand.

Let's run the playbook and take a look what it does.

```
$ ansible-playbook solutions/playbook __loops2.yml
PLAY [all]
*********************************************************
*********************************************************
****

TASK [Gathering Facts]
*********************************************************
***************************************************
ok: [node1.example.com]
ok: [node2.example.com]

TASK [Creating accounts]
*********************************************************
*************************************************
changed: [node1.example.com] => (item={u'comment':
u'DevOps Account', u'home': u'/home/devops', u'user':
u'devops'})
changed: [node1.example.com] => (item={u'comment':
u'Operator Account', u'home': u'/var/operator',
u'user': u'operator'})
changed: [node1.example.com] => (item={u'comment':
u'Technical Support', u'home': u'/home/techadm',
u'user': u'techadm'})

PLAY RECAP
*********************************************************
*********************************************************
****
```

```
node1.example.com            :
ok=2     changed=1    unreachable=0     failed=0
```

The result is 3 accounts created with different home folders and custom comments on node1. If you would try and solve it yourself without using list of hashes or list of dictionaries I would probably end up having 3 different tasks. And more variables you have, more complicated it will be.

Nested loops

When we need to iterate over the loops, one through other, 'with_nested' statement is available for us. Take a look at the example below:

```
$ cat solutions/playbook __loops3.1.yml
- hosts: node1.example.com
  tasks:
    - name: Creating empty files
      file:
        path: '/tmp/{{ item[0] }}-{{ item[1] }}'
        state: touch
      with __nested:
      - [ 'level1.1', 'level1.2', 'level1.3' ]
      - [ 'level2.1', 'level2.2' ]
```

Run the playbook:

```
$ ansible-playbook solutions/playbook __loops3.1.yml

PLAY [node1.example.com]
****************************************************************
*************************************************

TASK [Gathering Facts]
****************************************************************
*************************************************
ok: [node1.example.com]
```

```
TASK [Creating empty files]
*************************************************************
***********************************************
changed: [node1.example.com] => (item=[u'level1.1',
u'level2.1'])
changed: [node1.example.com] => (item=[u'level1.1',
u'level2.2'])
changed: [node1.example.com] => (item=[u'level1.2',
u'level2.1'])
changed: [node1.example.com] => (item=[u'level1.2',
u'level2.2'])
changed: [node1.example.com] => (item=[u'level1.3',
u'level2.1'])
changed: [node1.example.com] => (item=[u'level1.3',
u'level2.2'])

PLAY RECAP
*************************************************************
*************************************************************
****
node1.example.com             :
ok=2      changed=1      unreachable=0      failed=0
```

It takes first value in the first list and loops through all the values the second list. Then it takes second value and loops through all the values in the second list, and then does the same thing with third value in the first list. You can easily track the pattern when the playbook is being ran.

Now we are going to add one more level to this with_nested structure and check the behavior.

```
$ cat solutions/playbook __loops3.2.yml
- hosts: node1.example.com
  tasks:
    - name: Creating empty files
      file:
```

```
        path: '/tmp/{{ item[0] }}-{{ item[1] }}-{{
item[2] }}'
        state: touch
      with _nested:
      - [ 'level1.1', 'level1.2', 'level1.3' ]
      - [ 'level2.1', 'level2.2' ]
      - [ 'level3.1', 'level3.2' ]
```

Now carefully take a look at the results:

```
$ ansible-playbook solutions/playbook _loops3.2.yml

PLAY [node1.example.com]
*****************************************************************
************************************************

TASK [Gathering Facts]
*****************************************************************
*************************************************
ok: [node1.example.com]

TASK [Creating empty files]
*****************************************************************
**********************************************
changed: [node1.example.com] => (item=[u'level1.1',
u'level2.1', u'level3.1'])
changed: [node1.example.com] => (item=[u'level1.1',
u'level2.1', u'level3.2'])
changed: [node1.example.com] => (item=[u'level1.1',
u'level2.2', u'level3.1'])
changed: [node1.example.com] => (item=[u'level1.1',
u'level2.2', u'level3.2'])
changed: [node1.example.com] => (item=[u'level1.2',
u'level2.1', u'level3.1'])
changed: [node1.example.com] => (item=[u'level1.2',
u'level2.1', u'level3.2'])
changed: [node1.example.com] => (item=[u'level1.2',
u'level2.2', u'level3.1'])
```

```
changed: [node1.example.com] => (item=[u'level1.2',
u'level2.2', u'level3.2'])
changed: [node1.example.com] => (item=[u'level1.3',
u'level2.1', u'level3.1'])
changed: [node1.example.com] => (item=[u'level1.3',
u'level2.1', u'level3.2'])
changed: [node1.example.com] => (item=[u'level1.3',
u'level2.2', u'level3.1'])
changed: [node1.example.com] => (item=[u'level1.3',
u'level2.2', u'level3.2'])

PLAY RECAP
************************************************************
************************************************************
****
node1.example.com              :
ok=2     changed=1    unreachable=0    failed=0
```

The behavior is almost the same, the only difference now that it adds one more level to the hierarchy and loops through it. You can easily figure out the pattern if you compare the output of two previous playbooks.

And we may use as many lists in the 'with_nested' expression as we want. The number of complexity of course applies.

Looping over hashes

Sometimes we need to iterate over a complex structures with having access to its internals, we may use the 'with_dict' statement.

Check the playbook below.

```
$ cat solutions/playbook __loops4.yml
- hosts: node1.example.com
  become: yes
  tasks:
    - name: Creating accounts
```

```
        user: name='{{ item.key }}' comment='{{ item.
value.comment }}' shell='{{ item.value.shell }}'
      with__dict:
        devops:
            comment: DevOps User
            shell: /bin/bash
        operator:       .
            comment: Operator Account
            shell: /bin/sh
```

The result of playing this playbook is:

```
$ cat solutions/playbook__loops4.yml

PLAY [node1.example.com]
**********************************************************
***********************************************

TASK [Gathering Facts]
**********************************************************
***********************************************
ok: [node1.example.com]

TASK [Creating accounts]
**********************************************************
***********************************************
changed: [node1.example.com] => (item={'key':
u'operator', 'value': {u'comment': u'Operator Account',
u'shell': u'/bin/sh'}})
changed: [node1.example.com] => (item={'key':
u'devops', 'value': {u'comment': u'DevOps User',
u'shell': u'/bin/bash'}})

PLAY RECAP
**********************************************************
**********************************************************
****
```

```
node1.example.com          :
ok=2    changed=1    unreachable=0    failed=0
```

The above example shows that the top level variables 'devops' and 'operator' are treated as values of the 'item.key' variable and their keys the 'comment' and 'shell' are available as 'item.value.comment' and 'item.value.shell' variables. In short, the top level variables are accessible as 'item.key' and below values as 'item.value.<key>'.

Other loops expressions

There are several other statements which also iterate over lists of data.

Loop keyword	Description
with_file	Takes a list of control node file names. item is set to the content of each file in sequence
with_fileglob	Takes a file name globbing pattern. item is set to each file in a directory on the control node that matches that pattern, in sequence, non-recursively
with_sequence	Generates a sequence of items in increasing numerical order. Can take start and end arguments which have a decimal, octal, or hexadecimal integer value
with_random_choices	Takes a list. item is set to one of the list items at random

```
$ vagrant destroy --force
$ cd ../facts/
$ vagrant up
$ vagrant ssh-config > ~/.ssh/config
```

Facts

Facts are the information which Ansible gathers from managed hosts. Facts are accessible as regular variables and include information like this:

- Network settings: interfaces, IP addresses, routes, etc
- Hostname, domain name
- OS related information: type, version, kernel version
- Disk drives and filesystems information
- CPU and memory details
- Other host related information

Gathering facts

We mentioned earlier that there's a built-in task that gathers all the facts when you run your playbook. It calls gather_facts. By default, it is set to true, and Ansible, before executing any tasks, performs gathering facts from managed hosts specified in the "hosts" statement. If you do not use facts in your playbook it makes sense to disable 'gather_facts'. It will also speed up the overall performance.

```
- hosts: all
  gather _facts: yes
  tasks:
     ...
```

The setup module

When you specify 'gather_facts' statement in a playbook, Ansible executes the setup module. It is enabled by default and Ansible runs it automatically.

Before starting using facts, it is generally a good idea to check if Ansible is able to gather these facts from your managed hosts. In order to do this, we can use following ad-hoc command.

```
$ ansible -m setup node1.example.com
node1.example.com | SUCCESS => {
    "ansible _facts": {
        "ansible _all _ipv4 _addresses": [
            "10.0.2.15"
        ],
        "ansible _all _ipv6 _addresses": [
            "fe80::5054:ff:feca:e48b"
```

```
        ],
        "ansible_apparmor": {
            "status": "disabled"
        },
        "ansible_architecture": "x86_64",
        "ansible_bios_date": "12/01/2006",
        "ansible_bios_version": "VirtualBox",
        "ansible_cmdline": {
...
output truncated for brevity
...
```

When this ad-hoc command is run it gives an output in JSON format. Facts might be presented as string or integer values, lists, or dictionaries.

If you want to display only specific variables, you can use a filter argument of the setup module:

```
$ ansible -m setup node1.example.com -a
'filter=ansible_distribution'
node1.example.com | SUCCESS => {
    "ansible_facts": {
        "ansible_distribution": "CentOS"
    },
    "changed": false,
    "failed": false
}


$ ansible -m setup node1.example.com -a
'filter=ansible_eth0
ansible -m setup node1.example.com -a
'filter=ansible_eth0'
node1.example.com | SUCCESS => {
    "ansible_facts": {
        "ansible_eth0": {
            "active": true,
            "device": "eth0",
...
```

```
output truncated for brevity
...
```

```
                },
                "hw_timestamp_filters": [],
                "ipv4": {
                    "address": "10.0.2.15",
                    "broadcast": "10.0.2.255",
                    "netmask": "255.255.255.0",
                    "network": "10.0.2.0"
                },
                "ipv6": [
                    {
                        "address":
"fe80::5054:ff:feca:e48b",
                        "prefix": "64",
                        "scope": "link"
                    }
                ],
                "macaddress": "52:54:00:ca:e4:8b",
                "module": "e1000",
                "mtu": 1500,
                "pciid": "0000:00:03.0",
                "promisc": false,
                "speed": 1000,
                "timestamping": [
                    "tx_software",
                    "rx_software",
                    "software"
                ],
                "type": "ether"
            }
        },
        "changed": false,
        "failed": false
}
```

There are few ways of how to access all these values and use them in your playbooks. Take a look at the playbook below.

```
$ cat solutions/playbook2.1.yml
- hosts: node1.example.com
  become: yes
  gather _facts: yes
  tasks:
    - name: Set correct hostname
      hostname: name='{{ inventory _hostname }}'

    - name: Adding own IP address into /etc/hosts
file
      lineinfile:
        path: /etc/hosts
        regexp: '^{{ ansible _eth0.ipv4.address }}.*$'
        line: '{{ ansible _eth0.ipv4.address }} {{
inventory _hostname }}'

    - name: Install tcpdump package (CentOS only)
      yum: name='tcpdump' state=installed
      when: ansible _distribution == 'CentOS'
```

If we have complex variables which contain other enclosed variables like shown in the example above variable 'ansible_eth0.ipv4.address' they can be accessed by using dots '.'. Or you can use more pythonic way like ansible_eth0['ipv4']['address'], or even a combination of both like ansible_eth0['ipv4'].address.

Take a look at the example below.

```
$ cat solutions/playbook2.2.yml
- hosts: node2.example.com
  become: yes
  gather _facts: yes
  tasks:
    - name: Set correct hostname
      hostname: name='{{ inventory _hostname }}'

    - name: Adding own IP address into /etc/hosts file
      lineinfile:
```

```
        path: /etc/hosts
        regexp: "^{{ ansible_eth0['ipv4']['address']
}}.*$"
        line: "{{ ansible_eth0['ipv4']['address'] }}
{{ inventory_hostname }}"

    - name: Install tcpdump package (CentOS only)
      yum: name='tcpdump' state=installed
      when: ansible_distribution == 'CentOS'
```

The result of running both playbook will be the same.

```
$ ansible-playbook solutions/playbook2.1.yml
PLAY [node1.example.com]
************************************************************
*************************************************

TASK [Gathering Facts]
************************************************************
**********************************************
ok: [node1.example.com]

TASK [Set correct hostname]
************************************************************
*******************************************
changed: [node1.example.com]

TASK [Adding own IP address into /etc/hosts file]
************************************************************
*********************
changed: [node1.example.com]

TASK [Install tcpdump package (CentOS only)]
************************************************************
*************************
changed: [node1.example.com]
```

```
PLAY RECAP
***********************************************************
***********************************************************
****
node1.example.com          :
ok=4     changed=3     unreachable=0     failed=0

$ ansible-playbook solutions/playbook2.2.yml

PLAY [node2.example.com]
***********************************************************
**********************************************

TASK [Gathering Facts]
***********************************************************
*************************************************
ok: [node2.example.com]

TASK [Set correct hostname]
***********************************************************
*********************************************
changed: [node2.example.com]

TASK [Adding own IP address into /etc/hosts file]
***********************************************************
*********************
changed: [node2.example.com]

TASK [Install tcpdump package (CentOS only)]
***********************************************************
************************
changed: [node2.example.com]

PLAY RECAP
***********************************************************
**********************************************
****
```

```
node2.example.com          :
ok=4    changed=3    unreachable=0    failed=0
```

Keep in mind that different OS'es provide different sets of variables but most of them are still the same. Before referring to gathered facts just make sure that the facts available for a particular operating system type.

The set_fact module, dynamic facts

Sometimes during executing of playbooks we need to define variables dynamically. In these situations, you can use 'set_fact' module. Take a look at the example below.

```
$ cat solutions/playbook3.yml
- hosts: node1.example.com
  become: yes
  gather _facts: yes
  tasks:
    - name: Defining a custom variable
      set _fact:
        hostinfo: 'Host: {{ inventory _hostname }} /
IPaddr: {{ ansible _eth0.ipv4.address }}'
        other _var: 'MacAddr: {{ ansible _eth0.
macaddress }}'

    - name: Printing hostinfo variable
      debug: msg='{{ hostinfo }}'

    - name: Printing other _var variable
      debug: msg='{{ other _var }}''
```

Now run this playbook:

```
$ ansible-playbook solutions/playbook3.yml
PLAY [node1.example.com]
*****************************************************
*********************************************
```

```
TASK [Gathering Facts]
****************************************************
***********************************************
ok: [node1.example.com]

TASK [Defining a custom variable]
****************************************************
************************************
ok: [node1.example.com]

TASK [Printing hostinfo variable]
****************************************************
************************************
ok: [node1.example.com] => {
    "msg": "Host: node1.example.com / IPaddr:
10.0.2.15"
}

TASK [Printing other _var variable]
****************************************************
************************************
ok: [node1.example.com] => {
    "msg": "MacAddr: 52:54:00:ca:e4:8b"
}

PLAY RECAP
****************************************************
****************************************************
****
node1.example.com          :
ok=4    changed=0    unreachable=0    failed=0
```

The variables defined by using the 'set_fact' module work absolutely the same way as static variables and facts. So, we can easily access these facts using the debug module.

Managed nodes facts

Sometimes you need to have variables defined in files on managed nodes. This lets you to have for each of managed node an individual set of variables. In order to do this, create on each of managed nodes the /etc/ansible/facts.d/ directory and place there files which names end on the .fact extension. These files will be read automatically when the setup module runs.

The fact files may be written in either JSON or INI formats. These facts files may be even written in bash, python, perl, scripts or be binary programs. The only requirement is such scripts and programs should return output in JSON or INI format.

```
$ vagrant ssh node1.example.com
node1.example.com$ mkdir -p /etc/ansible/facts.d/
node1.example.com$ cat /etc/ansible/facts.d/
node1_facts.fact
[os_facts]
os_release=CentOS
os_version=7.4

[ip_facts]
eth0_ip=10.0.2.15
```

To access the facts we can use ah-hoc:

```
$ ansible -m setup node1.example.com -a
'filter=ansible_local'
node1.example.com | SUCCESS => {
    "ansible_facts": {
        "ansible_local": {
            "node1_facts": {
                "ip_facts": {
                    "eth0_ip": "10.0.2.15"
                },
                "os_facts": {
                    "os_release": "CentOS",
                    "os_version": "7.4.1708"
```

```
                    }
                }
            }
        },
        "changed": false,
        "failed": false
}
```

Instead of setting these facts manually we can use Ansible and save these facts to a file.

```
$ cat solutions/playbook4.yml
- hosts: node.example.com
  become: yes
  gather_facts: yes
  tasks:
    - name: create directory for custom facts
      file:
        path:  /etc/ansible/facts.d/
        recurse=yes
        state: directory

    - name: Creating custom facts file for custom os
release fact
      lineinfile:
        path: /etc/ansible/facts.d/
{{inventory_hostname}}.fact
        regexp: '{{ item.line }}'
        line: '{{ item.regexp }}'
      with_items:
        - { regexp: '\[os_facts\]', line:
'[os_facts]'}
        - { regexp: 'os_release*', line:
'os_release={{ansible_distribution}}'}
        - { regexp: 'os_version*', line:
'os_version={{ansible_distribution_version}}'}
        - { regexp: '\[ip_facts\]', line:
'[ip_facts]'}
```

```
        - { regexp: 'eth0 _ip', line: 'eth0 _ip={{
ansible _eth0["ipv4"]["address"] }}'}

    - name: gather new facts
      setup:

    - name: Printing hostinfo variable
      debug: msg='{{ ansible _local }}'
```

Running the playbook should give you the following results:

```
$ ansible-playbook solutions/playbook4.yml
PLAY [node2.example.com]
**********************************************************
*************************************************

TASK [Gathering Facts]
**********************************************************
************************************************
ok: [node2.example.com]

TASK [create directory for custom facts]
**********************************************************
******************************
changed: [node2.example.com]

TASK [Creating custom facts file for custom os
release fact]
**********************************************************
***********
changed: [node2.example.com] => (item={u'regexp': u'\\
[os _facts\\]', u'line': u'[os _facts]'})
changed: [node2.example.com] => (item={u'regexp':
u'os _release*', u'line': u'os _release=CentOS'})
changed: [node2.example.com] => (item={u'regexp':
u'os _version*', u'line': u'os _version=7.4.1708'})
changed: [node2.example.com] => (item={u'regexp': u'\\
[ip _facts\\]', u'line': u'[ip _facts]'})
```

```
changed: [node2.example.com] => (item={u'regexp':
u'eth0 _ip', u'line': u'eth0 _ip=10.0.2.15'})

TASK [do facts module to get latest information]
*****************************************************
***********************
ok: [node2.example.com]

TASK [Printing hostinfo variable]
*****************************************************
**************************************
ok: [node2.example.com] => {
    "msg": {
        "node2.example.com": {
            "ip _facts": {
                "eth0 _ip": "10.0.2.15"
            },
            "os _facts": {
                "os _release": "CentOS",
                "os _version": "7.4.1708"
            }
        }
    }
}


PLAY RECAP
*****************************************************
*************************************************
node2.example.com           :
ok=5    changed=2    unreachable=0    failed=0
```

Facts obtained this way absolutely have no difference from facts gathered by the gather_facts module.

Caching facts

When you have many hosts, gathering facts each time is a time-consuming operation. Ansible has a few mechanisms to save facts between running.

The configuration file ansible.cfg in the [defaults] section has several options regarding to the caching facts:

- gathering – type of caching to use
- fact_caching – format of cached facts
- fact_caching_connection – parameters for connecting to facts storage
- fact_caching_timeout – 86400

The 'gathering' option - default value is implicit, which means that facts will gathered each time when a playbook is run unless the gather_facts option set to False. Other possible value is explicit. It disables gathering facts unless the gather_facts options is set to True. Last possible value is smart. It allows Ansible to read other options fact_* to find out how to cache facts.

Some information about facts is available at the official website http://docs.ansible.com/ansible/latest/playbooks_variables.html.

Bring down your VMs and get ready for the new lab:

```
$ vagrant destroy --force
$ cd ../templates/
$ vagrant up
```

Templates

Templating is an essential part of Ansible. Templates give the possibility to distribute and modify text files on managed hosts. The most common usage of templates is to deploy configuration files.

Ansible uses Jinja2 template engine which is written like Ansible on Python language. This template engine is widely used in other programming languages, tools and applications.

Before we continue, just do quick introducing some basic constructions which is used in Jinja2.

Delimiters

When Jinja2 reads a text file it processes the only text which enclosed into special constructions:

```
{% ... %} - statements for operators like for, if, set,
etc, ...
{{ ... }} - to print variables' values
{# ... #} - interpreted as commentaries and ignored
```

Jinja2 does not allow mixing one type brackets within another.

Loops

Jinja2 uses the for operator to provide standard loop functionality:

```
{% set users = [ 'user1', 'user2', 'user3' ] %}
{% for user in users %}
{{ loop.index }}. Username: {{ user }}
{% endfor %}
```

The result of using this template would be:

```
0. Username: user1
1. Username: user2
2. Username: user3
```

We can see the **for .. in .. endfor** operator enclosed in the {% ... %} brackets. It tells Jinja2 to interpret the text inside as a control operator. The loop. index is another special variable which appears only inside the **for** operator and before the **endfor** keyword.

The **set** operator creates a new variable which is available only in a current template file.

Conditions

Jinja2 uses the **if .. else .. endif** statement to provide conditional control. Take a look at the example beow:

```
{% if inventory _hostname == "node1.example.com" %}
This text is appeared only if current managed host
is node1.example.com.
{% else %}
This text is appeared on all nodes but node1.
example.com.
{% endif %}
```

Few things to note here, inventory_hostname is used without any quotes because it is a variable, and "node1.example.com" is within the brackets because it is a string.

After the **if** keyword follows a statement that should evaluate into a boolean value. Multiple statements might be combined into a single by using **AND** and **OR** operands. In the **if .. else .. endif** construction only the **if .. endif** part is mandatory. And this will be processed only if a statement returns True. The keyword **.. else ..** is optional. After it executes expressions if a statement returns False.

The conditional expression may also include so many **elif** statements as needed to check multiple conditions.

To evaluate statements you may use and combine following operators.

Operator	Description	Example
==	Equal	"{{ max_memory }} == 512"
<	Less than	"{{ min_memory }} < 128"`
>	Greater than	"{{ min_memory }} > 256"

Operator	Description	Example
<=	Less than or equal to	"{{ min_memory }} <= 256"`
>=	Greater than or equal to	"{{ min_memory }} >= 512"
!=	Not equal to	"{{ min_memory }} != 512"
is defined	Variable exists	"{{ min_memory }} is defined"
is not defined	Variable does not exist	"{{ min_memory }} is not defined"
<variable>	Variable is set to 1, True, or yes if its value defined and not equal None, 0, False, empty	"{{ available_memory }}"
not <variable>	Variable is set to 0, False, or no	"not {{ available_memory }}"
<variable> in <array>	Value is present in a variable or an array	"{{ users }} in users["db_admins"]"
expr1 and expr2	Evaluates to True if both expr1 and expr2 are true	True and 5
expr1 and expr2	Evaluates to True if any of expr1 and expr2 is true	False or True

The above operators are used inside of the {% ... %} brackets.

The template module

Ansible is shipped with the **template** module which passes text files (templates) via Jinja2 template engine and then copies the result to managed hosts.

This module works almost the same as the **copy** module with additional Jinja2 processing.

```
$ cat hosts.j2
127.0.0.1        localhost
{{ ansible _eth0.ipv4.address }} {{
inventory _hostname }}

$ cat solutions/playbook1.yml
- hosts: all
  become: yes
  tasks:
    - name: Set modified /etc/hosts file
      template:
        src: ../hosts.j2
        dest: /etc/hosts
```

The file hosts.j2 is written to be processed by Jinja2. Playbook1.yml includes the task to process this template and deploy it on node1 and node2.

Before we run our playbook, check the content of hosts file on both nodes:

```
$ ssh node1.example.com 'cat /etc/hosts'; ssh node2.
example.com 'cat /etc/hosts'
127.0.0.1   localhost localhost.localdomain
localhost4 localhost4.localdomain4
::1         localhost localhost.localdomain
localhost6 localhost6.localdomain6

127.0.0.1   localhost localhost.localdomain
localhost4 localhost4.localdomain4
::1         localhost localhost.localdomain
localhost6 localhost6.localdomain6
```

Now run the playbook:

```
$ ansible-playbook solutions/playbook1.yml
PLAY [all]
```

```
**********************************************************
**********************************************************
****

TASK [Gathering Facts]
**********************************************************
*************************************************
ok: [node1.example.com]
ok: [node2.example.com]

TASK [Set modified /etc/hosts file]
**********************************************************
***********************************
changed: [node1.example.com]
changed: [node2.example.com]

PLAY RECAP
**********************************************************
**********************************************************
****
node1.example.com            :
ok=2     changed=1    unreachable=0     failed=0
node2.example.com            :
ok=2     changed=1    unreachable=0     failed=0
```

After running the playbook1.yml the results will be:

```
$ ssh node1.example.com `cat /etc/hosts'; ssh node2.
example.com `cat /etc/hosts'
127.0.0.1        localhost
10.0.2.15 node1.example.com

127.0.0.1        localhost
10.0.2.15 node2.example.com
```

In the following example we are going to bring **for** operation into the picture

```
$ cat hosts2.j2
127.0.0.1    localhost
{% for host in groups['all'] %}
{{ hostvars[host].ansible _eth0.ipv4.address }} {{
hostvars[host].inventory _hostname }}
{% endfor %}

$ cat solutions/playbook2.yml
- hosts: all
  become: yes
  tasks:
    - name: Set modified /etc/hosts file
      template:
        src: ../hosts2.j2
        dest: /etc/hosts
```

Run the playbook2.yml:

```
$ ansible-playbook solutions/playbook2.yml

PLAY [all]
*************************************************************
*************************************************************
****

TASK [Gathering Facts]
*************************************************************
***************************************************
ok: [node2.example.com]
ok: [node1.example.com]

TASK [Set modified /etc/hosts file]
*************************************************************
**********************************
changed: [node2.example.com]
changed: [node1.example.com]
```

```
PLAY RECAP
*************************************************************
*************************************************************
****
node1.example.com          :
ok=2    changed=1    unreachable=0    failed=0
node2.example.com          :
ok=2    changed=1    unreachable=0    failed=0
```

After running the playbook2.yml the results will be:

```
$ ssh node1.example.com `cat /etc/hosts'; ssh node2.
example.com `cat /etc/hosts'
127.0.0.1    localhost
10.0.2.15 node1.example.com
10.0.2.15 node2.example.com

127.0.0.1    localhost
10.0.2.15 node1.example.com
10.0.2.15 node2.example.com
```

You will be able to find more information about templating and templates at http://docs.ansible.com/ansible/latest/playbooks_templating.html and http://docs.ansible.com/ansible/latest/template_module.html

The copy module

Sometimes you need to create small files with several lines of text. Using the template module in such cases is an excess way because of having a separate template file. You can use the **copy** module in these situations. This module allows you to put the files content directly defining it in playbooks. See the example below:

```
$ cat solutions/playbook4.yml

- hosts: all
  become: yes
```

```
    tasks:

      - name: setup MOTD on the VM
        copy:
          content: |
            Host Information
            ----------------
            Hostname             : {{
inventory_hostname }}
            Distribution         : {{
ansible_distribution }}
            OS Version           : {{
ansible_distribution_version }}
            Kernel Version       : {{ ansible_kernel }}
            Architecture         : {{
ansible_architecture }}
            Primary IP Address : {{
ansible_default_ipv4.address }}
            Memory Size          : {{
ansible_memory_mb.real.total }} MB total / {{
ansible_memory_mb.real.free }} MB free
            Disk Drive           : {{ ansible_devices.
sda.model }} / {{ ansible_devices.sda.size }}
          dest: /etc/motd
          owner: root
          group: root
          mode: 0755
```

Run this playbook:

```
$ ansible-playbook solutions/playbook4.yml

PLAY [all]
***********************************************************
***************************************************

TASK [Gathering Facts]
***********************************************************
```

```
***************************************************
ok: [node1.example.com]
ok: [node2.example.com]

TASK [Placing the Message Of Day file /etc/motd (the
copy module)]
*********************************************************
*****
changed: [node2.example.com]
changed: [node1.example.com]

PLAY RECAP
*********************************************************
***************************************************
node1.example.com          :
ok=2     changed=1     unreachable=0     failed=0
node2.example.com          :
ok=2     changed=1     unreachable=0     failed=0
```

And verify the results:

```
$ ssh node1.example.com cat /etc/motd; ssh node2.
example.com cat /etc/motd

Host Information
----------------
Hostname            : node1.example.com
Distribution        : CentOS
OS Version          : 7.4.1708
Kernel Version      : 3.10.0-693.5.2.el7.x86 __64
Architecture        : x86 __64
Primary IP Address  : 10.0.2.15
Memory Size         : 488 MB total / 272 MB free
Disk Drive          : VBOX HARDDISK / 40.00 GB

Host Information
----------------
Hostname            : node2.example.com
```

```
Distribution        : CentOS
OS Version          : 7.4.1708
Kernel Version      : 3.10.0-693.5.2.el7.x86_64
Architecture        : x86_64
Primary IP Address  : 10.0.2.15
Memory Size         : 488 MB total / 272 MB free
Disk Drive          : VBOX HARDDISK / 40.00 GB
```

Bring down your VMs and get ready for the new lab

```
$ vagrant destroy --force
$ cd ../filters/
$ vagrant up
```

Filters

Sometimes, before a variable is being used, its value need to be modified. Filters can help in that. Filters are the functions that used for modifying values in templates and tasks. Ansible is shipped within several filters along with ones that implemented in Jinja2 templating engine. Common syntax while using filters is:

```
{{ variable | filter }}
{{ variable | filter(arg1, arg2, …) }}
{{ variable | filter1 | filter2 | … }}
```

Filters are used to modify a value contained in a variable. We can call several filters one after the other using pipe "|"method . Take a look at the example below.

```
$ cat solutions/playbook1.yml
- hosts: node1.example.com
  become: yes
  tasks:
    - name: Processing values before copying a file
      copy:
        content: |
```

This demonstrates some capabilities of filters

    {{ '1. Removing whitespaces' | replace(' ', '') }}

    {{ undefvar | default('2. Create a variable and set a default value to it') }}

    3. Getting a random number in 0..100 {{ 100 | random }}

    4. Getting a unique items from a list {{ ['one', 'one', 'two', 'one', 'three'] | unique }}

    5. An average value of two minimums {{ ([5, 3, 2, 6, 8]|min + [9, 17, 5, 3]|min)/2 }}

    6. Power of 5 by 5 is {{ 5 | pow(5) }}

    7. Test if a given string is an IP address 127.0.0.1 = {{ '127.0.0.1' | ipv4 }}

    8. Getting a SHA1 hashsum of 'Hello, World!' {{ 'Hello, World!' | hash('sha1') }}

    9. Combining a list of items into a string {{ ['', 'usr', 'share', 'doc', 'ansible'] | join('/') }}

    10. Calling several filters at once {{ 2 | pow(2) | root(2)*10 }}
   dest: /tmp/filters.txt

Run this playbook:

```
$ ansible-playbook solutions/playbook1.yml

PLAY [node1.example.com]
***********************************************************
***********************************************

TASK [Gathering Facts]
***********************************************************
*************************************************
ok: [node1.example.com]
```

```
TASK [Processing values before copying a file]
********************************************************
************************
changed: [node1.example.com]

PLAY RECAP
********************************************************
********************************************************
****
node1.example.com              :
ok=2     changed=1    unreachable=0     failed=0
```

After running you should see the following result:

```
$ ssh node1.example.com cat /tmp/filters.txt

This demonstrates some capabilities of filters
1.Removingwhitespaces
2. Create a variable and set a default value to it
3. Getting a random number in 0..100 45
4. Getting a unique items from a list ['one', 'two',
'three']
5. An average value of two minimums 2.5
6. Power of 5 by 5 is 3125.0
7. Test if a given string is an IP address 127.0.0.1
= 127.0.0.1
8. Getting a SHA1 hashsum of 'Hello, World!'
0a0a9f2a6772942557ab5355d76af442f8f65e01
9. Combining a list of items into a string /usr/
share/doc/ansible
10. Calling several filters at once 20.0
```

More information about filters is available at http://docs.ansible.com/ansible/latest/playbooks_filters.html.

Bring down your VMs and get ready for the new lab

```
$ vagrant destroy --force
$ cd ../roles/
$ vagrant up
```

Roles

Roles is one more way to organize your tasks. You may have as many playbooks as you want but it will become unmanageable at some point.

Role is a repeatable code that can be run multiple times with or without
passing any arguments when you run it. Role is a library which does one
or multiple things when called. Role is not a replacement for a playbook,
but rather an addition to it.

A structure of a role

Ansible.cfg file has a special variable under the [defaults] section which
calls 'roles_path'. If you do not have this option specified then Ansible looks
for roles directory in your current path. You can also change this value and
set this path to something else.

Take a look at the example below

```
.
├── ansible.cfg
├── inventory
└── roles
    └── role1
        ├── defaults
        │   └── main.yml
        ├── files
        │   └── file1
        ├── handlers
        │   └── main.yml
        ├── tasks
        │   └── main.yml
        ├── templates
        │   └── nginx.conf.j2
```

```
└── vars
        └── main.yml
```

In the example 'role1' is a name of our custom role. The **default, files, handlers, meta, tasks, templates,** and **vars** are standard directories of our 'role1'. Directories **default, handlers, tasks,** and **vars** must have a main.yml file inside because Ansible looks up for main.yml file when calling a role. You may also create and use your custom files by using the **include** and **include_vars** statements in the role1/tasks/main.yml file. All subdirectories are optional except **tasks**. It is logical since all other directories are called from tasks/main.yml file.

Directories **defaults** and **vars** are almost the same but have different priorities.

The **files** directory is usually referred by the **copy** module when files are copied to managed hosts. The same behavior is done for the **template** module.

Playbooks vs Roles

Although a role looks like a playbook it has a few distinctions. One of them is that a playbook definition includes a list of managed hosts, and role just includes a list of tasks. Check the table below:

A typical playbook	A role's task: tasks/main.yml

- hosts: list of hosts
  tasks:
  - module1: ...
  - module2: ...
  - ...
	- module1: ...
	- module2: ...
	- module3: ...

As we can see, tasks defined in a role includes only tasks. And playbook consist of several sections like 'hosts' and 'tasks', and can also include 'vars', 'become' and others Ansible keywords we already discussed.

Role Wordpress

Let us take a look at a simple role which installs and configures Wordpress, a popular site engine. First, check the working directory structure.

```
$ tree .
.
├── Vagrantfile
├── ansible.cfg
├── inventory
├── roles
│   └── wordpress
│       ├── defaults
│       │   └── main.yml
│       ├── handlers
│       │   └── main.yml
│       ├── tasks
│       │   ├── configure __mariadb.yml
│       │   ├── configure __nginx.yml
│       │   ├── configure _php.yml
│       │   ├── configure __wordpress.yml
│       │   ├── install.yml
│       │   └── main.yml
│       └── templates
│           ├── nginx.conf.j2
│           └── wp-config.php.j2
├── site1.yml
└── site2.yml
```

Take a look at site1.yml playbook content :

```
$ cat site1.yml
- hosts: all
  become: true
  roles:
  - wordpress
```

119

While processing, Ansible looks for **roles/tasks/defaults/main.yml** file and registers all the variables found there. This file contains some common variables which are specified in tasks/main.yml file of role1:

```
$ cat roles/wordpress/defaults/main.yml
install _packages:
- nginx
- php-fpm
- mariadb-server
- wordpress
- MySQL-python
wordpress _dbname: wordpress
wordpress _dbuser: wordpress
wordpress _dbpass: VeRYH3AvYP@$sW0RD
```

Then **tasks/mail.yml** file is being read:

```
$ cat roles/wordpress/tasks/main.yml
- name: Checking whether a managed host runs CentOS
  assert:
    that: ansible _distribution == 'CentOS'
    msg: This role supports only CentOS

- include _tasks: install.yml
- include _tasks: configure _nginx.yml
- include _tasks: configure _php.yml
- include _tasks: configure _mariadb.yml
- include _tasks: configure _wordpress.yml
```

This playbooks, or rather list of tasks is being processed as usual playbook.

Pre and post tasks

Sometimes you need to run simple tasks alongside with roles, in order to avoid writing roles for simple tasks, we can use pre and post tasks:

```
$ cat solutions/site2.yml
- hosts: all
```

```
    become: true
    pre _tasks:
    - name: Set correct hostname
      hostname: name='{{ inventory _hostname }}'
    post _tasks:
    - name: Add an operator account
      user: name=operator
    roles:
    - wordpress

$ cat roles/wordpress/tasks/main.yml
- name: Checking whether a managed host runs CentOS
  assert:
      that: ansible _distribution == 'CentOS'
      msg: This role supports only CentOS

- include _tasks: install.yml
- include _tasks: configure _nginx.yml
- include _tasks: configure _php.yml
- include _tasks: configure _mariadb.yml
- include _tasks: configure _wordpress.yml

$ cat roles/wordpress/tasks/install.yml
- name: Install epel repository
  yum: name=epel-release state=present
  when: ansible _distribution == 'CentOS'

- name: Install packages (CentOS only)
  yum: name='{{ item }}' state=present
  with _items: '{{ install _packages }}'
  when: ansible _distribution == 'CentOS'

$ cat roles/wordpress/tasks/configure _*
- name: Make sure that MariaDb server is running
  service: name='mariadb' state=running enabled=on

- name: Create a database
  mysql _db:
```

```
        name: '{{ wordpress__dbname }}'

- name: Create a database user
  mysql__user:
    name: '{{ wordpress__dbuser }}'
    password: '{{ wordpress__dbpass }}'
    priv: '{{ wordpress__dbname }}:ALL'

- name: Configure Nginx
  template:
    src: nginx.conf.j2
    dest: /etc/nginx/nginx.conf
    validate: /usr/sbin/nginx -t -c %s
  notify:
    - Reload Nginx

- name: Make sure that Php-Fpm is running
  service: name=php-fpm state=running enabled=on

- name: Configure wordpress
  template:
    src: wp-config.php.j2
    dest: /etc/wordpress/wp-config.php
    owner: root
    group: apache
    mode: '0640'
  notify:
  - Reload Nginx
```

The **pre_tasks** and **post_tasks** are sections which allows us to run some tasks before and after running roles.

Run the playbook and check the results:

```
$ ansible-playbook solutions/site2.yml
```

```
PLAY [all]
*********************************************************
*************************************************

TASK [Gathering Facts]
***********************************************************
***************************************************
ok: [node1.example.com]

TASK [Set correct hostname]
***********************************************************
***********************************************
ok: [node1.example.com]

TASK [wordpress : Checking whether a managed host
runs CentOS]
***********************************************************
***********
ok: [node1.example.com] => {
    "changed": false,
    "failed": false,
    "msg": "All assertions passed"
}

TASK [wordpress : include_tasks]
***********************************************************
*****************************************
included: /Users/dzuev/Dropbox/Books/ansible_book/
chapter_3/roles/roles/wordpress/tasks/install.yml
for node1.example.com

TASK [wordpress : Install epel repository]
***********************************************************
*****************************
ok: [node1.example.com]
```

```
TASK [wordpress : Install packages (CentOS only)]
*************************************************************
***********************
changed: [node1.example.com] => (item=[u'nginx',
u'php-fpm', u'mariadb-server', u'wordpress',
u'MySQL-python'])

TASK [wordpress : include_tasks]
*************************************************************
****************************************
included: /Users/dzuev/Dropbox/Books/
ansible_book/chapter_3/roles/roles/wordpress/tasks/
configure_nginx.yml for node1.example.com

TASK [wordpress : Configure Nginx]
*************************************************************
*************************************
changed: [node1.example.com]

TASK [wordpress : include_tasks]
*************************************************************
*****************************************
included: /Users/dzuev/Dropbox/Books/ansible_book/
chapter_3/roles/roles/wordpress/tasks/configure_php.
yml for node1.example.com

TASK [wordpress : Make sure that Php-Fpm is running]
*************************************************************
*********************
changed: [node1.example.com]

TASK [wordpress : include_tasks]
*************************************************************
*******************************************
included: /Users/dzuev/Dropbox/Books/
ansible_book/chapter_3/roles/roles/wordpress/tasks/
configure_mariadb.yml for node1.example.com
```

```
TASK [wordpress : Make sure that MariaDb server is
running]
**********************************************************
**************
changed: [node1.example.com]

TASK [wordpress : Create a database]
**********************************************************
************************************
changed: [node1.example.com]

TASK [wordpress : Create a database user]
**********************************************************
******************************
changed: [node1.example.com]

TASK [wordpress : include _tasks]
**********************************************************
******************************************
included: /Users/dzuev/Dropbox/Books/
ansible _book /chapter _3/roles/roles/wordpress/
tasks/configure _wordpress.yml for node1.example.com

TASK [wordpress : Configure wordpress]
**********************************************************
***********************************
changed: [node1.example.com]

RUNNING HANDLER [wordpress : Reload Nginx]
**********************************************************
****************************
changed: [node1.example.com]

TASK [Add an operator account]
**********************************************************
*******************************************
ok: [node1.example.com]
```

```
PLAY RECAP
*********************************************************
*********************************************************
******
node1.example.com          :
ok=18    changed=8    unreachable=0    failed=0
```

From the output above, we can see that first "Set correct hostname" pre-task section was run, then all the tasks from the role 'wordpress' and finally, the task 'Add an operator account' from post-task section.

Bring down your VMs and get ready for the new lab

```
$ vagrant destroy --force
$ cd ../vault/
$ vagrant up
```

Vault

Ansible Vault manages data in encrypted files. Check ansible-vault syntax:

```
$ ansible-vault [create|decrypt|edit|encrypt|rekey]
[options] file _name
```

```
Options:
--vault-password-file=FILE          allows to specify
an encrypted file's password in a passwordfile instead
of a command line
--new-vault-password-file=FILE includes a new password
when rekeying an encrypted file
```

```
Subcommands:
create         - creates a new encrypted file
decrypt        - removes the encryption, after that
a file stops be secured
edit           - editing an encrypted file
encrypt        - makes a plain text file encrypted
```

```
rekey            - changes a password of an encrypted
file
```

There is no built-in password database in Ansible, and working with version control systems like git requires keeping all the variables including some sensitive data in there. It is not safe to keep this kind of data as clear text. To solve that problem, we can use Ansible vault and encrypt files containing this data. Let's start with some basic

```
$ tree
.
├── Vagrantfile
├── ansible.cfg
├── host _vars
│   ├── node1.example.com
│   └── node1.example.com.plain
├── inventory
└── solutions
    └── playbook1.yml
```

Take a look at the playbook:

```
$ cat solutions/playbook1.yml
- hosts: all
  become: true
  tasks:
  - name: create user1
    user:
      name: "{{username}}"
      password: "{{ password |
password _hash('sha512') }}"
```

You can see that we have 'username' and 'password' variables specified. Their values are kept in the separate hosts_vars directory and look like below:

```
$ cat host _vars/node1.example.com
username: user1
password: user1 _pass
```

Currently this data is kept in the clear text. We are going to use Ansible vault to encrypt this file.

```
$ ansible-vault encrypt host_vars/node1.example.com
New Vault password:  [VERYSTRONGPASSWORD]
Confirm New Vault password:
[VERYSTRONGPASSWORD_AGAIN]
Encryption successful
```

File host_vars/node1.example.com.yml will be encrypted at this point and you won't be able to read this data in clear text more through regular text viewers.

```
$ cat host_vars/node1.example.com
$ANSIBLE_VAULT;1.1;AES256
6163326435333163613062373738303466376563643565333330530
62373837393435643463138
363633663635336461303230363930316432363338373134 0a356332
31353566353939373433346634
39366430353396531353832633538346463435303064346465323633
626130393637366662613532
6164363666366231320a3936333306264323131376431656364633334
63666635343239366537661
38393635396434633438363834666563393433330434306564393232632
306636386637623063313665
36356261646465386361663431616237323765533631666465
```

Now, if we try to run the run_nginx_role.yml playbook, it will fail as in the example below:

```
$ ansible-playbook solutions/playbook1.yml
ERROR! Attempting to decrypt but no vault secrets
found
```

Since this file has been encrypted we must provide vault password to decrypt the data:

```
$ ansible-playbook solutions/playbook1.
yml --ask-vault-pass
Vault password:

PLAY [all]
*************************************************************
*************************************************************
******

TASK [Gathering Facts]
*************************************************************
********************************************************
ok: [node1.example.com]

TASK [create user1]
*************************************************************
*****************************************************
changed: [node1.example.com]

PLAY RECAP
*************************************************************
*************************************************************
******
node1.example.com              :
ok=2    changed=1    unreachable=0    failed=0
```

Ansible-vault command works with YAML formatted files so you can encrypt any files with variables and playbooks.

Ansible-vault can encrypt even binary files. When we need to copy some files that we store locally encrypted to managed servers in plain text the Copy module does it. So when you run a playbook with encrypted data just make sure that the access data were correctly supplied.

In order to edit vault encrypted files you can execute the following command:

```
$ ansible-vault edit host _vars/node1.example.com
Vault password:
Confirm New Vault password:

-------------------------------
username: user1
password: user1 _pass
```

Few things to keep in mind:

- Make sure that you do not lose the vault password, otherwise you won't be able to decrypt and lose all the data within.
- You can use as many encrypted files as you want, but make sure to use the same password

Bring down your VMs and get ready for the new lab

```
$ vagrant destroy --force
$ cd ../error _handling/
$ vagrant up
```

Error handling

Ansible has built-in checks when processing the task results and smart enough to identify the error if any, but in some situations, it is not the case, especially if you use 'raw', 'shell' or 'command' modules. This section describes how to change the default behavior of Ansible when handling certain errors.

By default, if a task fails, your playbook will exit with an error. This behavior can be overridden by skipping failed tasks. For that you can use **ignore_errors** statement.

```
$ cat solutions/playbook1.yml
---
- hosts: all
  become: true
```

```
  tasks:
    - yum: name=wrongpackagename state=present
#      ignore_errors: yes

    - name: Installing a correct package
      yum: name=tcpdump state=present
```

Run the playbook:

```
$ ansible-playbook solutions/playbook1.yml
PLAY [all]
****************************************************************
****************************

TASK [Gathering Facts]
****************************************************************
*****************
ok: [node1.example.com]

TASK [yum]
****************************************************************
****************************
fatal: [node1.example.com]: FAILED! => {"changed":
false, "failed": true, "msg": "No package matching
'wrongpackagename' found available, installed or
updated", "rc": 126, "results": ["No package matching
'wrongpackagename' found available, installed or
updated"]}
      to retry, use: --limit @/Users/dzuev/Dropbox/
Books/ansible_book/chapter_3/error_handling/
playbook1.retry

PLAY RECAP
****************************************************************
****************************
node1.example.com            :
ok=1    changed=0    unreachable=0    failed=1
```

131

Now uncomment "ignore_errors: yes" line, the result will be different:

```
$ ansible-playbook solutions/playbook1.yml
PLAY [all]
***********************************************************
****************************

TASK [Gathering Facts]
***********************************************************
****************

ok: [node1.example.com]

TASK [yum]
***********************************************************
****************************

fatal: [node1.example.com]: FAILED! => {"changed":
false, "failed": true, "msg": "No package matching
'wrongpackagename' found available, installed or
updated", "rc": 126, "results": ["No package matching
'wrongpackagename' found available, installed or
updated"]}
...ignoring

TASK [Installing a correct package]
***********************************************************
****

changed: [node1.example.com]

PLAY RECAP
***********************************************************
****************************

node1.example.com              :
ok=3    changed=1    unreachable=0    failed=0
```

The first task fails because of there is no the package named 'wrongpacka-
gename' but the playbook will continue to run.

By default, if a task which handler statement fails, then handler will fail as well. We can override this behavior by using the **force_handlers** statement. It forces the handler to be called even if the task fails. The following example shows how to use the force_handlers statement:

```
$ cat solutions/playbook2.yml
---
- hosts: all
  force _handlers: yes
  become: true
  tasks:
    - yum: name=mariadb state=latest
      notify: restart _database

  handlers:
    - name: restart _database
      service:
        name: mariadb
        state: restarted
```

Run the playbook:

```
$ ansible-playbook solutions/playbook2.yml
PLAY [all]
*************************************************************
***************************
TASK [Gathering Facts]
*************************************************************
*****************
ok: [node1.example.com]

TASK [yum]
*************************************************************
**************************
changed: [node1.example.com]
```

```
RUNNING HANDLER [restart__database]
**************************************************
*****
fatal: [node1.example.com]: FAILED! => {"changed":
false, "failed": true, "msg": "Could not find the
requested service mariadb: host"}
      to retry, use: --limit @/Users/dzuev/Dropbox/
Books/ansible__book/chapter__3/error__handling/
playbook2.retry

PLAY RECAP
**************************************************
****************************
node1.example.com            :
ok=2    changed=1    unreachable=0    failed=1
```

If you want to change the criteria for failed task, there is **failed_when** statement available. The following example shows how **failed_when** statement can be used:

```
$ cat solutions/playbook3.yml
---
- hosts: all
  force__handlers: yes
  become: true
  tasks:
    - script: create__users.sh
      register: command__result
#      failed__when: "'Password is missing' in
command__result.stdout"

    - name: Fail task when the command error output
prints FAILED
      command: /usr/bin/std__err.sh
      register: command__result
#      failed__when: not (command__result.stderr ==
0 or command__result.stderr == 12)
```

Error handling with blocks

In playbooks, blocks are set of tasks within 'tasks' statement. Blocks allow for logical grouping of tasks, and can be used to control how tasks are executed. For example, administrators can define a main set of tasks and a set of extra tasks that will only be executed if the first set of tasks fails. Blocks have three main components:

- **block**: Defines the main tasks to run.
- **rescue**: Defines the tasks that will be run if the tasks defined in the block clause fails.
- **always**: Defines the tasks that will always run independently of the success or failure of tasks defined in the block and rescue clauses.

The following example shows how to implement a block in a playbook. Even if tasks defined in the **block** clause fail, tasks defined in the **rescue** and **always** clauses will be executed:

```
$ cat solutions/playbook4.yml
---
- hosts: all
  tasks:
    - block:
        - shell: echo "This is the main block"
      rescue:
        - shell: echo "This block runs if main block
fails"
      always:
        - shell: echo "This block runs always"
```

By default if certain task fails on one host, it will still run on the other hosts specified in the playbook. If you want to override this behavior, you can use **any_errors_fatal** statement in the hosts section:

```
- hosts: all
  any _errors _fatal: true
  roles:
    - role1
```

If there is a need to run your playbooks through a certain set of tasks which can tolerate a few fails, you can use **max_fail_percentage** statement.

```
- hosts: all
  max _fail _percentage: 50
  roles:
    - role1
```

Chapter 4. Best Practices

Ansible is a very flexible and very powerful tool and depending on how you use it, it can be either like a silver bullet or a daily headache in your automation journey. There are several things about Ansible you need to remember:

- Ansible does not require a special server for running
- Ansible is cross-platform and supported by pretty much any OS or appliance.
- Ansible is clientless, which mean you do not need a special server.
- Ansible utilizes SSH, the industrial standard, to access to managed hosts
- Ansible is easily extensible by custom filters and modules
- Ansible inventory sources might be specified statically or provided dynamically

Keeping Ansible under version control

Make sure that you keep your Ansible files and projects under version control. It has several benefits:

- All changes are tracked.
- A version control system is also considered as a backup solution for Ansible files and projects
- It allows you to work in a team and collaborate more efficiently

Git allows to every engineer has a local copy and work locally in and, in meantime, a central repository is a primary source. Even if you don't have a Git server, having a local repository is a big plus although you should take care about backing it up on you own.

Where to keep Ansible files

By default Ansible looks for a configuration file, inventory, etc. in the /etc/ ansible directory if running Linux (other OSs might use different paths) and the /etc directory usually is not writable for the users. So, make sure that you have Ansible.cfg and inventory files separate per project or have a dedicated servers single inventory path. One of the examples would be using Ansible Tower.

Managing inventories

There is the inventory option in the ansible.cfg file which specifies where inventory file or directory is. While you inventory contains a small amount of groups or hosts, using a single file is an easy way to manage the hosts. More groups will be added in the inventory, more confusing it will get. The best you can do is split your inventory into different hosts and groups files or even use dynamic inventories. Dynamic inventories are out of scope and not being covered in this book.

Managing facts

Once you have playbooks written and they run on a regular basis, gathering facts is getting to be a bottleneck that slow down the initial starting of tasks. In large environments, it makes sense to allocate a caching server, so every time you run a playbook Ansible looks up for specific in a database. It takes less time and has much better performance. You have to set a proper lifetime for cached facts and configure a playbook to run the gathering facts at nights, this allows to keep facts refreshed during the business hours.